W9-ATT-809

Summary of Contents

EVERYTHING YOU KNOW ABOUT CSS IS WRONG!

BY **RACHEL ANDREW**
& KEVIN YANK

Everything You Know About CSS Is Wrong!

by Rachel Andrew and Kevin Yank

Copyright © 2008 SitePoint Pty. Ltd.

Managing Editor: Chris Wyness

Technical Editor: Andrew Tetlaw

Technical Director: Kevin Yank

Printing History:

    First Edition: October 2008

Editor: Hilary Reynolds

Index Editor: Russell Brooks

Cover Design: Alex Walker

Published by SitePoint Pty. Ltd.

48 Cambridge Street
Collingwood VIC Australia 3066
Web: www.sitepoint.com
Email: business@sitepoint.com

ISBN 978-0-9804552-2-9
Printed and bound in Canada

About Rachel Andrew

Rachel Andrew is a web developer and the director of web solutions provider edgeofmyseat.com. When not writing code, she writes *about* writing code and is the coauthor of several books promoting the practical usage of web standards alongside other everyday tools and technologies. Rachel takes a common-sense, real-world approach to web standards, with her writing and teaching being based on the experiences she has in her own company every day.

Rachel lives in the UK with her partner Drew and daughter Bethany. When not working, they can often be found wandering around the English countryside hunting for geocaches and nice pubs that serve Sunday lunch and a good beer.

About Kevin Yank

As Technical Director for SitePoint, Kevin Yank keeps abreast of all that is new and exciting in web technology. Best known for his book *Build Your Own Database Driven Website Using PHP & MySQL*, now in its third edition, Kevin also writes the *SitePointTech Times*, a free weekly email newsletter that goes out to over 150,000 subscribers worldwide.

When he isn't speaking at a conference or visiting friends and family in Canada, Kevin lives in Melbourne, Australia; he enjoys flying light aircraft and performing improvised comedy theater with Impro Melbourne. His personal blog, *Yes, I'm Canadian*, can be found at http://yesimcanadian.com/.

About the Technical Editor

Andrew Tetlaw has been tinkering with web sites as a web developer since 1997. Before that, he worked as a high school English teacher, an English teacher in Japan, a window cleaner, a car washer, a kitchen hand, and a furniture salesman. He is dedicated to making the world a better place through the technical editing of SitePoint books and kits. He is also a busy father of five, enjoys coffee, and often neglects his blog at http://tetlaw.id.au/.

About SitePoint

SitePoint specializes in publishing fun, practical, and easy-to-understand content for web professionals. Visit http://www.sitepoint.com/ to access our books, newsletters, articles, and community forums.

Table of Contents

Chapter 5   The Road Ahead

Preface

It's been over ten years since I first started to build web sites. Ten years isn't a long period of time, but when it comes to the Web and web browsers, much water has passed under the bridge in the last decade. I can remember when Netscape 4 and Internet Explorer 4 brought us exciting new ways to embellish our web pages. I can also remember, all too clearly, the pain of trying to support Netscape 4 as the rest of the Web moved on.

Our current situation with Internet Explorer 6 reminds me of those days of wanting to move forward and use CSS for layout while also trying to support the ailing Netscape 4. On the one hand, we know that there is still a significant number of users using Internet Explorer 6; on the other, we know how much more potential we could have, and how much easier our lives would be, if we weren't forced to patch up our sites with alternate style sheets to cope with that dinosaur.

In this book, we take a good look at what's just around the corner with the impending launch of Internet Explorer 8. The layout methods that I'll demonstrate in this book aren't new; they have been included in browsers such as Safari, Firefox, and Opera for a good while. However, the launch of Internet Explorer 8 will tip the balance in favor of these under-utilized techniques. Now is the perfect time to take stock of the current methods considered best practice for CSS layout, and determine how they can be improved upon.

Updating and refining the techniques we use to build web sites is part of the business of working on the Web, wherever you stand on the utility of CSS tables. This book is an opinionated book, written to inspire debate and experimentation in a time of change and development.

With the long-awaited launch of Internet Explorer 8 not far away, it is time for us all to rediscover CSS.

Who Should Read This Book?

This is not your average book about CSS. This book is aimed at web designers and developers who:

- need to work with CSS layouts—from those just beginning to those who possess a good working knowledge of CSS layout techniques

- have a desire to stay ahead and keep their CSS knowledge fresh and relevant

- want to explore the future possibilities provided by increasing levels of CSS compatibility in modern browsers

For these web professionals, this book should be required reading.

What's in This Book?

Chapter 1: The Problem with CSS

Chapter 1 sets the scene for what will be a milestone for CSS compatibility in browsers: the arrival of Internet Explorer 8. Here, we explore the current problems with CSS layout techniques, as well as the mismatch between what designers want and what CSS provides.

Chapter 2: CSS Table Layout

Chapter 2 is all about CSS layout techniques. We first explain the current techniques that use absolute positioning and floated elements, and the complexity involved in getting them to work reliably. We then introduce CSS tables, spend some time exploring how CSS tables work, and provide some examples of how easily they can be used to create a grid-based layout. This is the chapter that will put the final nail in the coffin of HTML table-based layouts.

Chapter 3: CSS Table Solutions

In this chapter, we test the limits of what CSS tables can do, explore the edge cases, and deliver concrete solutions. After your initiation into the science of CSS tables, you will probably be bursting with those "But, how do I…" questions—this chapter seeks to answer them for you.

Chapter 4: Considering Older Browsers

Is the use of CSS tables an unreachable Utopian dream? This chapter will convince you that CSS table-based layouts are ready for prime time by providing practical solutions for supporting IE6 and 7.

Chapter 5: The Road Ahead

While CSS tables can be used today, what's around the corner? CSS3 will provide a substantial increase in layout control, and this chapter is a preview of what's to come. We take a detailed look at three CSS3 modules for layout control: the multi-column layout module, the grid-positioning module, and the template layout module.

The Book's Web Site

Located at http://www.sitepoint.com/books/csswrong1/, the web site that supports this book will give you access to the following facilities:

The Code Archive

As you progress through this book, you'll note a number of references to the code archive. This is a downloadable ZIP archive that contains each and every line of example source code that's printed in this book. If you want to cheat (or save yourself from carpal tunnel syndrome), go ahead and download the archive.[1]

Updates and Errata

No book is perfect, and we expect that watchful readers will be able to spot at least one or two mistakes before the end of this one. The Errata page on the book's web site (http://www.sitepoint.com/books/csswrong1/errata.php) will always have the latest information about known typographical and code errors.

The SitePoint Forums

If you'd like to communicate with us or anyone else on the SitePoint publishing team about this book, you should join SitePoint's online community.[2] The CSS

---

[1] http://www.sitepoint.com/books/csswrong1/code.php
[2] http://www.sitepoint.com/forums/

forum, in particular, can offer an abundance of information beyond the solutions in this book.[3]

In fact, you should join that community even if you don't want to talk to us, because a lot of fun and experienced web designers and developers hang out there. It's a good way to learn new stuff, get questions answered in a hurry, and just have fun.

The SitePoint Newsletters

In addition to books like this one, SitePoint publishes free email newsletters, including *The SitePoint Tribune* and *The SitePoint Tech Times*. Reading them will keep you up to date on the latest news, product releases, trends, tips, and techniques for all aspects of web development. Sign up to one or more SitePoint newsletters at http://www.sitepoint.com/newsletter/.

Your Feedback

If you can't find an answer through the forums, or if you wish to contact us for any other reason, the best place to write to is books@sitepoint.com. We have a well-staffed email support system set up to track your inquiries, and if our support team members are unable to answer your question, they'll send it straight to us. Suggestions for improvements, as well as notices of any mistakes you may find, are especially welcome.

Conventions Used in This Book

You'll notice that we've used certain typographic and layout styles throughout this book to signify different types of information. Look out for the following items:

Code Samples

Code in this book will be displayed using a fixed-width font, like so:

```
<h1>A perfect summer's day</h1>
<p>It was a lovely day for a walk in the park. The birds
were singing and the kids were all back at school.</p>
```

---

[3] http://www.sitepoint.com/forums/forumdisplay.php?f=53

If the code may be found in the book's code archive, the name of the file will appear at the top of the program listing, like this:

```
                                                              example.css
.footer {
  background-color: #CCC;
  border-top: 1px solid #333;
}
```

If only part of the file is displayed, this is indicated by the word *excerpt*:

```
                                                    example.css (excerpt)
  border-top: 1px solid #333;
```

If additional code is to be inserted into an existing example, the new code will be displayed in bold:

```
function animate() {
  new_variable = "Hello";
}
```

Also, where existing code is required for context, rather than repeat all the code, a vertical ellipsis will be displayed:

```
function animate() {
  ⋮
  return new_variable;
}
```

Some lines of code are intended to be entered on one line, but we've had to wrap them because of page constraints. A ➡ indicates a line break that exists for formatting purposes only, and should be ignored:

```
URL.open("http://www.sitepoint.com/blogs/2007/05/28/user-style-she
➡ets-come-of-age/");
```

Tips, Notes, and Warnings

 ### Hey, You!

Tips will give you helpful little pointers.

 ### Ahem, Excuse Me ...

Notes are useful asides that are related—but not critical—to the topic at hand. Think of them as extra tidbits of information.

 ### Make Sure You Always ...

... pay attention to these important points.

 ### Watch Out!

Warnings will highlight any gotchas that are likely to trip you up along the way.

Acknowledgments

Thanks to the team at SitePoint, and particularly Kevin Yank for his contributions to this book. In the course of writing this book, I have become even more aware of how much we lowly web developers owe to those who write the specifications and build the browsers. So thanks to those unsung heroes, in particular the people within browser companies who really do understand web standards and work to produce the best browsers possible. Finally, as always, grateful thanks to my long-suffering family for enduring yet another book project.

Chapter 1

The Problem with CSS

I'm a visionary. I'm ahead of my time. Trouble is, I'm only about an hour and a half ahead.
—George Carlin

The problem with CSS is that CSS is too hard.

There. We got that out of the way easily enough, didn't we? You can skip to Chapter 2 now.

Okay, maybe that was a little unfair. For the most part, **Cascading Style Sheets** (CSS) technology is beautiful in its elegance and simplicity. It gives web designers a language in which to describe a consistent visual treatment that can be applied to a single page, an entire site, or even a whole *bunch* of sites. Yes, CSS was ahead of its time when it was first created, but it didn't stay that way for long.

As CSS was conceived in an age when the design of most web sites still looked quite plain, its creators couldn't anticipate the richness and intricacy of the designs that it would eventually be asked to describe. And so the Web marched inexorably on, while CSS struggled to catch up. Clever designers figured out ways to make CSS do what they needed it to do, but these techniques were so convoluted that they quickly became difficult for the rest of us to master.

These techniques were also quite fragile. Since they employed CSS features in creative and unexpected ways, their use tended to expose the subtle inconsistencies and limitations of the CSS support in each of the major browsers. Today, even the most experienced designers routinely see their sites break in new and unpredictable ways as a result of a subtle change in content, or a new browser release.

For the creative elite who came up with these often mind-bending techniques, CSS can offer a thrilling and constantly surprising landscape in which to work. But for beginners learning to design their first web sites, today's CSS can be shockingly difficult to work with. CSS is just too hard.

The good news is, that's all about to change.

Whether you consider yourself a CSS layout expert, have previously tried to learn CSS layout techniques and given up in frustration, or are only just exploring CSS for the first time, *everything you know about CSS is wrong.*

The Grid's the Thing

For better or worse, most web design is based around two-dimensional (2D) grids. Talented designers have ways of making these grid-based designs look less "boxy," but with very few exceptions, the grid is always underneath the frills and furbelows.

Unfortunately, CSS was not designed to describe 2D grids. Rather, CSS assumes that every page will be made up of a vertical stack of **blocks**, piled one on top of another, each containing either another stack of blocks, or text (called **inline content**) wrapped to fit inside the block.

Take Figure 1.1, the SitePoint homepage. This page is divided into a header, a footer, and the body content. Each of these components is a block; if a given block doesn't occupy the full width of the browser window, whatever space is left over will appear as empty whitespace to either side. This example shows the kind of one-dimensional layout that CSS was designed to describe; if that's all there was to the layout of the site, well, CSS would be perfectly equipped to describe it, and I wouldn't be writing this book!

Figure 1.1. sitepoint.com as a one-dimensional layout

Of course, that *isn't* all there is to the layout of sitepoint.com, nor is a vertical stack of blocks an adequate model for describing almost any web page designed in the past decade. Invariably, when designing a site, you want to arrange blocks side by side.

Let's look more closely at the structure of the SitePoint homepage. In Figure 1.2, you can see the grid that describes the layout of the page. In particular, notice the number of blocks that sit alongside another block. Every single one represents an element of the page that will require the designer to employ some degree of trickery to make CSS do something it wasn't designed to do.

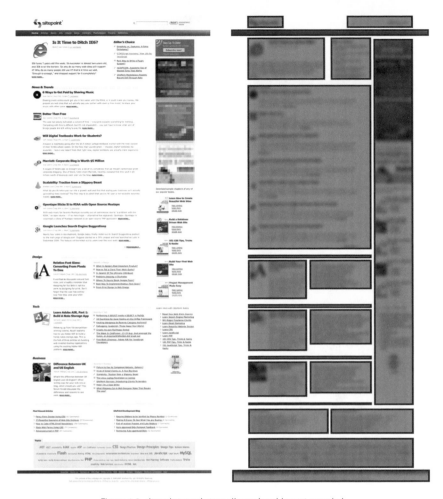

Figure 1.2. sitepoint.com's two-dimensional layout revealed

When many designers sit down to lay out a new web site, one of the first steps they will take is to draw a grid. Try visiting a few of your favorite sites—play a little "spot the grid." It's usually not difficult to see.

Shortly after early browsers like Internet Explorer 3 added support for CSS, it became abundantly clear to designers that CSS wasn't up to the task of building the 2D grids needed to achieve the rich layouts they wanted. Good old HTML, however, offered a feature that obviously could do the job: **HTML tables**.

Tables Do the Trick

Designers seized on the HTML `table` element as a page layout tool. Rather than reserving it for its designated purpose—the display of spreadsheet-like tables of data—designers found that they could stick the blocks of their pages into table cells, forming the two-dimensional grids they craved.

By the time the `table` element made it into the official HTML specification with HTML 3.2 in 1997,[1] it was already being used extensively as a page layout device, having been included in web browsers since Netscape 1.1 and Internet Explorer 1. See Figure 1.3 for an example of an early tables tutorial.

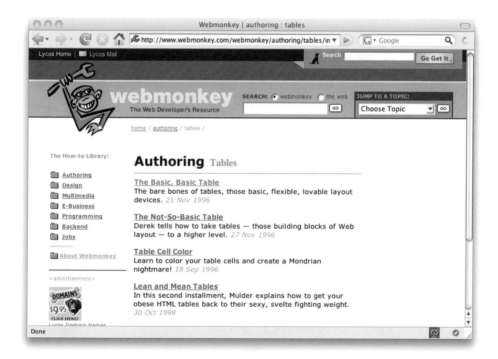

Figure 1.3. Tables tutorials on the popular Webmonkey site

The HTML language, originally conceived to describe the structure of academic documents, was now being used as a page layout language—a usage for which it

---

[1] http://www.w3.org/TR/REC-html32

was entirely unsuited. Nevertheless, it worked; at the time, this was more than could be said for page layout with CSS.

While designers plied their trade with HTML tables, the Web's brightest minds understood that something had to change. The Web had the potential to be presented and navigated not just by the large monitors of desktop computers, but on portable devices with smaller screens, in non-visual browsers designed for visually disabled people, and by search engines and other computer programs that crawl the Web for information. But that potential would never be realized as long as HTML elements like `table` were being used to achieve visual layout tasks, rather than to provide meaningful information that could be conveyed by non-visual browsers.

Within the design community, many clever designers also saw this potential. Through years of experimentation, they found ways to make CSS reach beyond its limited sphere. As we'll see in Chapter 2, it turns out that features like **absolute positioning** and **floated blocks** can be employed to force blocks to sit alongside other blocks—a purpose never envisioned by its creators.

These techniques have formed the basis of many books about CSS, including several of my own previous titles, such as *HTML Utopia: Designing Without Tables Using CSS, 2nd Edition.*[2] Although these features have been tried and tested, and are in use on most professionally-designed sites today, I wouldn't describe them as stable, predictable, or easy to use.

But now there's a new arrival in the world of CSS—it's about to render those books obsolete, and transform the arcane art of CSS layout into a simple discipline easy enough for almost anyone to adopt.

CSS and the Browser Wars

So what kept designers from embracing CSS page layout for so many years? Well, it wasn't the initial shortcomings of CSS. It was the inability for CSS to grow fast enough to keep up with the needs of web designers.

More specifically, the state of CSS *support* in web browsers hadn't kept up.

---

[2] http://www.sitepoint.com/books/css2/

Even *more* specifically, Internet Explorer dropped the ball by resting on its laurels while the other major browsers continued their work to improve the layout capabilities of CSS.

Early Browser Support for CSS

Internet Explorer 3, released on August 14, 1996, was the first commercial browser with any support for the fledgling CSS specification.[3] Microsoft released a CSS Gallery, pictured in Figure 1.4, in order to show off some of the new layout control enabled by CSS.

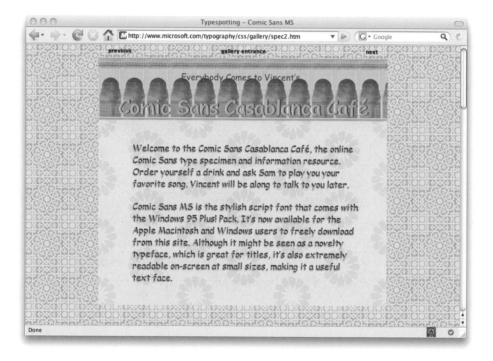

Figure 1.4. A page in the CSS Gallery, showing CSS support in IE3

In retrospect, it's extraordinary just how quickly developments were taking place at this point. Microsoft announced that CSS would be part of Internet Explorer 3 even while discussions were still underway as to which style sheet language should be used on the Web. Furthermore, Microsoft had an implementation of the language

---

[3] http://www.w3.org/Style/CSS/msie/

in its browser *before* the official recommendation was published by the World Wide Web Consortium (W3C).

At first, Microsoft's main competitor, Netscape, took a wait-and-see attitude towards CSS, and focused instead on extending HTML, adding new tags with each release of the browser. For example, Netscape submitted its proposal for frames to the W3C in September 1995, but then implemented the idea in the browser before any real discussion had taken place about the addition.

This continual flow of innovation and drive to push features into browsers was stimulating the Web's development, and enhancing the agency of page authors and designers. However, the addition of features to a web browser actually entailed changing the path of the Web itself, and two browser vendors attempting to go about it in different ways promised trouble.

The year 1997 saw the launch of the version 4 browsers … and the start of the browser wars.

The Version 4 Browsers

Netscape 4 was released in June 1997, with Internet Explorer 4's arrival lagging slightly behind in October. Both browsers offered reasonable support for the CSS1 specification, at least where styling text was concerned, and developers were able to begin working with CSS. Developer adoption of the most basic parts of CSS was relatively quick, not least because both Netscape and Internet Explorer 4 included support for Dynamic HTML (DHTML)—using JavaScript to manipulate the Document Object Model of a page and CSS.

Netscape's legacy as an early web browser was beginning to show. Microsoft had rebuilt its rendering engine for IE4—using the Trident engine, which continues to be used in browsers up to and including IE8—whereas Netscape was adding CSS and DHTML support on top of the existing browser codebase. This meant that as developers pushed the limits of CSS in the version 4 browsers, numerous strange bugs started to emerge.

Internet Explorer began to attract market share away from Netscape; the release of IE5 in 1999, with much-improved CSS support, cemented this trend. By early 2000, IE had pulled ahead to claim over 50% of the browser market share.

Internet Explorer 6 and the Long Sleep

Internet Explorer 6 was released in August 2001, and, with the dominance established by IE5—and the general lack of interest in the new Gecko-based Netscape 6—Microsoft's ultimate victory was guaranteed in the browser wars.

Internet Explorer 6 was a good browser in its day. Its CSS support was mature enough for persistent designers to be able to achieve most page layout tasks, if they pushed the support to its limits. There were some peculiar bugs, but for those of us who had battled with Netscape 4 for years, they seemed fairly trivial. Microsoft had even released a version of Internet Explorer 5 for the Macintosh, which featured a brand new rendering engine with dramatically better CSS support than any previous Microsoft browser. Meanwhile, the W3C was working to define additions to CSS that promised to make page layout a cinch. The future was bright.

The problem was what Microsoft did—or didn't do—next. Having produced a browser that made web developers relatively happy, which let them do most of the things they thought they needed to do at the time, and having effectively won the browser wars, Microsoft shut down its browser development and reallocated the team members to other projects. Internet Explorer fell asleep.

Once IE's hibernation became apparent, many of us thought that the general population would start moving to other browsers. Firefox, based on Mozilla, had come onto the scene, and was more lightweight and robust than Netscape had ever managed. Opera had developed a browser with excellent CSS support and many other features, such as the first tabbed browsing interface. However, the general population saw that blue "e" as *the* Internet. Microsoft had created Internet Explorer simply as part of the operating system—the part that accessed the Internet—to the point that, even now, many regular web users are surprised to learn that there are other browser options.

Disappointed by Internet Explorer's stagnation, the web development community took to alternative browsers such as Firefox, and was quick to point out where IE6 was lacking. As Firefox, Apple's newly developed Safari, and that scrappy upstart Opera improved their browsers with every release, adding the unimplemented parts of CSS2.1 and fixing problematic bugs, the knowledge that IE6 wasn't being improved to offer the same degree of standards compliance became more and more frustrating to web designers everywhere.

Firefox began to draw closer to Microsoft in the market share race, reaching around 11% market share by July 2007, and showed no signs of slowing down. This increase was partly due to evangelism from the web community, and a strong marketing campaign, but also because of the growing number of security problems reported with Internet Explorer 6. To gain that amount of market share, Firefox's popularity had obviously spread beyond the web design community. Microsoft responded by announcing in February 2005 that a new version of Internet Explorer was to be released. The first beta version of IE7 became available in July 2005—almost four years after the release of Internet Explorer 6.

Internet Explorer 8 Changes the Game

Microsoft's announcement that it had resumed development of Internet Explorer attracted the attention of a grassroots organization formed in support of web standards: the Web Standards Project.[4] This standards body saw the opportunity to lobby Microsoft to include the CSS features needed to make page layout achievable by anyone, not just persistent experts. Thus, April 12, 2005, saw the birth of the Acid2 test.[5]

This test was designed to test CSS1 compliance in browsers, as did the original Acid Test.[6] The original Acid Test had been successful in demonstrating the limitations of the browsers of the time, and demonstrating what would be possible if those limitations were removed. This time, the focus was on CSS2. Håkon Wium Lie—the test author (and CTO of Opera software)—challenged Microsoft via a ZDNet article[7] to release Internet Explorer 7 as a browser that reached the tested standards.

At that time, no browser fully satisfied the demands of this test, but Internet Explorer was by far the worst off, results-wise. By the end of that year, Safari, Opera, and the Linux/KDE browser Konqueror had released versions supporting Acid2.

Internet Explorer 7 was finally released on October 18, 2007—*without* support for the features tested by Acid2. Acid2 support was too great a leap for Microsoft to make in a single release, but it had made significant progress. Some of the truly

---

[4] http://www.webstandards.org/

[5] http://www.webstandards.org/action/acid2/

[6] http://www.w3.org/Style/CSS/Test/CSS1/current/test5526c.htm

[7] http://news.zdnet.com/2100-9588_22-5620423.html

bizarre bugs had been fixed, and some useful CSS properties from the CSS2.1 specification were now present in the browser. Whether you love or hate the browser, the IE7 release meant Microsoft was back in the game—with a browser that made an attempt to support web standards in a meaningful way.

Meanwhile, developers were actively promoting browsers such as Firefox on their personal sites. Designers would often add little touches viewable only in favored non-IE browsers. The question on everybody's lips was that if Internet Explorer went back to sleep—now that IE7 had been launched and dealt with some of the biggest criticisms leveled at IE6—would we ever be able to enjoy some of the innovations made possible by a fuller implementation of CSS2.1, never mind CSS3?

Thankfully, the web community didn't have too long to wait after the release of IE7 before it became apparent that there was another version of Internet Explorer in development. In December 2007, the existence of Internet Explorer 8 was confirmed on the IEBlog.[8] On December 19, a post to the IEBlog[9] confirmed that IE8 rendered the Acid2 test correctly, letting web developers everywhere know that the CSS2 properties we had long wished for would finally be part of Internet Explorer 8.

Once the first beta of Internet Explorer 8 was made available in March 2008, we were all able to see it for ourselves—the smiling face of an Acid2 test pass, shown in Figure 1.5!

---

[8] http://blogs.msdn.com/ie/archive/2007/12/05/internet-explorer-8.aspx

[9] http://blogs.msdn.com/ie/archive/2007/12/19/internet-explorer-8-and-acid2-a-milestone.aspx

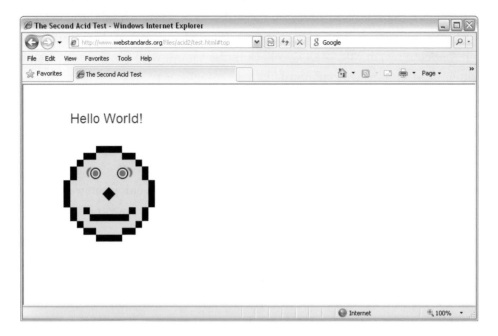

Figure 1.5. Internet Explorer 8 rendering the Acid2 test correctly

An Internet Explorer that offers near-full support for CSS2 opens up vast possibilities. Until now, designers who build sites for mainstream users have had to steer clear of CSS2 features that could make page layout stable, predictable, and a whole lot easier, just because Internet Explorer didn't support them. IE8 is a complete game-changer.

Over the last five or six years, we've seen many of the handcrafted CSS layouts and templates that we've created for clients transformed back into table-based layouts for one primary reason: the only people who get CSS are those that already know it. Invariably, HTML tables creep back into applications and web sites because their grid is easy to understand and doesn't require what may seem to be endless hours of fussing about to get things looking just right.

Don't get me wrong, CSS has helped improve the accessibility of an incredible number of sites and applications. But using something simpler, easier to understand, and that is designed specifically for the layout of a page or application can go a long way towards removing the perceived need for HTML tables for layout. When this happens, we all win, including people with accessibility needs.[10]

—Derek Featherstone[11]

Our Part of the Bargain

For years, we in the web design community have bemoaned the state of CSS support in Internet Explorer, and the limited (and, in many cases, buggy) set of tools it gave us. Page layout with CSS was a black art that rarely worked perfectly, predictably, or reliably, even for its most experienced practitioners.

After Internet Explorer's long sleep, Microsoft has finally responded with a browser that passes the Acid2 test, providing us with all the tools we've been demanding. With the imminent release of IE8, Microsoft has fulfilled its part of the bargain; now it's time to fulfil ours.

It's time for us to abandon the arcane CSS layout techniques we worked so hard to develop while Internet Explorer lay dormant. It's time for us all to learn and begin using the new CSS, lest Internet Explorer decide the time is right for another nap. It's time to embrace new ways of web design practice, seizing the new features that IE8 now joins the other major browsers in supporting. It's time for us to show the

---

[10] Photo courtesy of Aaron Gustafson, 2007

[11] http://boxofchocolates.ca/

beginners who are just now learning to design web pages for the first time that CSS *isn't* too hard anymore.

In the next chapter, I'll show you exactly how one particular CSS feature new in IE8 suddenly makes the most common CSS page layout tasks a piece of cake.

2

CSS Table Layout

When released, Internet Explorer 8 will support many new values for the CSS `display` property, including the table-related values: `table`, `table-row`, and `table-cell`—and it's the last major browser to come on board with this support. This event will mark the end of complex CSS layout techniques, and will be the final nail in the coffin of using HTML tables for layout. Finally, producing table-like grid layouts using CSS will be quick and easy.

Applying table-related `display` property values to web page elements causes the elements to mimic the display characteristics of their HTML table equivalents. In this chapter, I'll demonstrate how this will have a huge impact on the way we use CSS for web page layouts. However, before we can understand why CSS tables will be so useful to us, we need to have a quick look at current popular CSS layout methods and the problems we have with them.

Using Current Layout Techniques

As mentioned in Chapter 1, in order to coerce what effectively consists of a vertical stack of block elements into a grid-like layout, CSS authors have used absolute positioning or floating to force blocks to sit alongside each other. These techniques, while thoroughly tested in all modern browsers, are complex and not without problems. So let's have a quick review of how to build a simple three-column layout—such as the one shown in Figure 2.1—using current techniques.

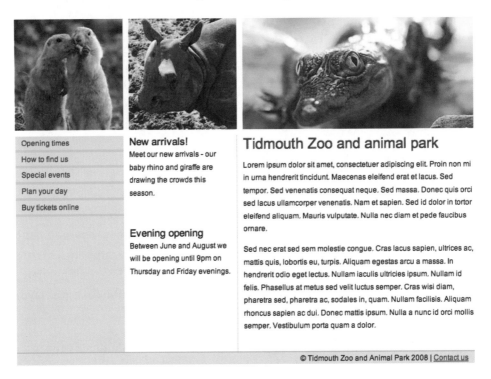

Figure 2.1. The layout we want to create

Here's an excerpt of the XHTML markup we'll be using to create this web page for the Tidmouth Zoo and Animal Park, showing the major structural elements:

```
<!DOCTYPE html PUBLIC "-//W3C//DTD XHTML 1.0 Strict//EN"
    "http://www.w3.org/TR/xhtml1/DTD/xhtml1-strict.dtd">
<html xmlns="http://www.w3.org/1999/xhtml" lang="en-US">
  <head>
    ⋮ HTML head content…
  </head>
  <body>
    <div id="wrapper">
      <div id="header">
        ⋮ top graphic banner…
      </div>
      <div id="main">
        <div id="content">
          ⋮ main article content…
        </div>
        <div id="nav">
          ⋮ navigation column content…
        </div>
        <div id="extras">
          ⋮ news headlines column content…
        </div>
      </div>
      <div id="footer">
        ⋮ page footer content…
      </div>
    </div>
  </body>
</html>
```

You'll be able to view the complete code and all supporting files for the page by downloading the code archive for this book from the SitePoint web site.[1]

Absolute Positioning

The first technique is to use **absolute positioning**. This is one of the more common layout techniques used today, and probably the easiest to implement. This layout works by making space for the two narrower columns, giving the main content area a large left margin, then positioning the two columns on top of the margin. We'll

---

[1] http://www.sitepoint.com/books/csswrong1/

focus on the CSS required for the layout of the major structural elements, but the complete CSS is available in the code archive.

We begin by setting a `width` for the `wrapper` div element, setting a `height` and background width for the `header` div, and defining the appearance of the `footer` div:

3col-absolute.css *(excerpt)*

```css
#wrapper {
  position: relative;
  text-align: left;
  width: 760px;
  margin-right: auto;
  margin-left: auto;
}
#header {
  height: 180px;
  background-image: url(images/header.jpg);
  background-repeat: no-repeat;
  padding-bottom: 10px;
}
#footer {
  border-top: 2px solid #d7ad7b;
  background-color: #e7dbcd;
  font-size: 80%;
  padding: 0.2em 10px 0.2em 0;
  text-align: right;
}
```

The `main` div is the parent element for our main content area and the two narrow columns. First, we'll relatively position the `main` div and then give the `content` div a left margin wide enough to fit the two other columns:

3col-absolute.css *(excerpt)*

```css
#main {
  position: relative;
}
#content {
  margin-left: 380px;
}
```

If we check out the layout in a browser, we'll see Figure 2.2—the content column is sitting nicely over to the right-hand side, leaving a `380px` left margin, which is where we'll place the other two columns.

Figure 2.2. Content column with space left for other columns

The final step is to absolutely position the two remaining columns within the space provided by the content `div`'s left margin:

```
                                                3col-absolute.css (excerpt)

#nav {
  position: absolute;
  top: 0;
  left: 0;
  width: 180px;
  background-color: #e7dbcd;
}
#extras {
  position: absolute;
  top: 0;
  left: 190px;
  width: 180px;
}
```

An absolutely positioned element is positioned relative to its closest positioned ancestor. In our case, the `main div` has been relatively positioned, so our two columns are positioned relative to its position in the page layout. Figure 2.3 shows how the absolutely positioned three-column layout appears in Firefox.

Problems with This Technique

As you can see in Figure 2.3, the background color of the `nav` column only extends as far as the content allows, whereas our original design calls for a full-length column.

We can circumvent this issue by adding a background image to the container element of the columns. This technique is described as **faux columns**, popularized in a well-known Alistapart article by Dan Cederholm.[2]

---

[2] http://www.alistapart.com/articles/fauxcolumns

Figure 2.3. The absolutely positioned layout in Firefox

In the case of our web page, the main div wraps all three columns, so we can add a background image to that element and position the image to appear behind the nav column—giving the appearance of a full-height column. The image also includes the dotted border that appears along the right-hand edge of the extras column. We achieve this effect in CSS by positioning the image shown in Figure 2.4 as a background image that repeats vertically.

Figure 2.4. The background image

All we need to do is add a couple of extra declarations to our style sheet:

```
                                            3col-absolute.css (excerpt)

#main {
  position: relative;
  background-image: url(images/main-bg.gif);
  background-repeat: repeat-y;
}
```

The result is the full-height column shown in Figure 2.5.

Figure 2.5. The finished absolutely positioned layout in Firefox

While all seems fine with the current layout, another problem arises if the content in the content column ends up shorter than the content of the nav column. As demonstrated in Figure 2.6, the footer will end up displaying across the content of all the columns instead of at the bottom of the page.

The reason for this problem is that absolutely positioning an element will remove it from the document flow. In our layout above, we've removed the two left-hand columns from the document flow and placed them on top of the other elements. The `content` and `footer` elements remain within the document flow, and are positioned by the browser under the `content div`.

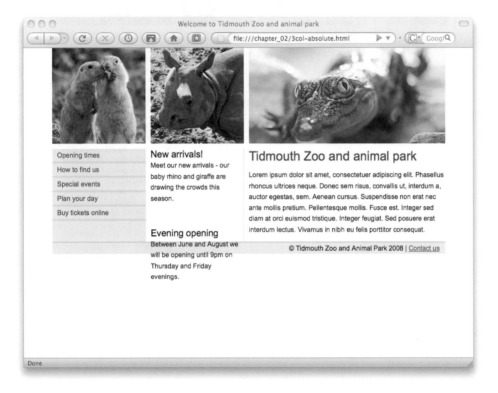

Figure 2.6. The footer problem

To combat this problem, you can add a top margin to the `footer` element, or bottom padding to the `content` element, to ensure the footer is an appropriate distance from the content. Neither of these options are particularly desirable; ideally, we'd like our footer to sit neatly under our content. However, beggars can't be choosers; if you can't guarantee the amount of content in the main content column, you may need to consider these approaches.

Finally, if you view this layout in Internet Explorer 6, you'll notice a big problem. The `nav` and `extras` columns aren't positioned correctly, as you can see in Figure 2.7.

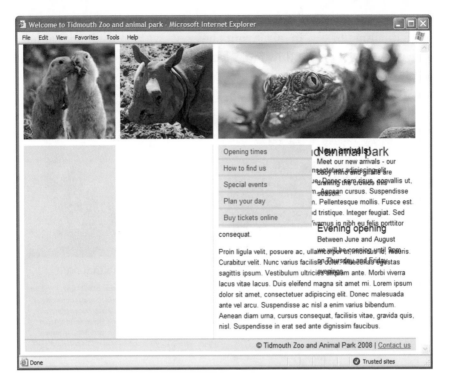

Figure 2.7. Layout problem in IE6

If we add the following `width` declaration to our style sheet, IE6 will be able to display our layout correctly:

```
                                           3col-absolute.css (excerpt)

#main {
  position: relative;
  width: 100%;
  background-image: url(images/main-bg.gif);
  background-repeat: repeat-y;
}
```

The above `width` declaration is in fact redundant, as we've also specified widths for all the columns; however, in this situation, it's a safe way to correct the layout in IE6 without affecting the layout in any other browser.

A Note on Internet Explorer and `hasLayout`

In Internet Explorer 6 and 7, applying a `width` declaration to an element causes the element to "gain a layout." It's far beyond the scope of this book to explain what gaining a layout means and why it's important in Internet Explorer—to put it in a nutshell, it means the `main div` will look after the layout of its child elements if it has a layout.

When an element has a layout, IE6 and 7's magical `hasLayout` property is set to `true`. There are other ways to trigger this property, including valid actions such as setting a `height` or floating the element, as well as those that involve adding IE-specific properties that don't validate, such as setting the `zoom` property to 1. If the concept of `hasLayout` is new to you, you might like to have a look at The SitePoint CSS Reference[3]—you'll find IE6 and 7 bugs far easier to deal with, once you understand the concept.

Floated Layout

The alternative to absolute positioning is a floated layout; by using the CSS `float` property, we can cause the column `div` elements to float alongside each other. We only need to make these few small changes to our CSS to turn our absolutely positioned layout into a floated layout:

3col-float.css (excerpt)

```css
#nav {
  float: left;
  margin-right: 10px;
  width: 180px;
  background-color: #e7dbcd;
}
#extras {
  float: left;
  width: 180px;
}
#content {
  float: right;
  width: 380px;
}
```

---

[3] http://reference.sitepoint.com/css/haslayout

Using the CSS `float` property, we've specified that the `nav` and `extras` columns will be floated to the left-hand side, while the `content` column will be floated to the right-hand side.

Problems with This Technique

If we test the layout after making those changes, we discover the disaster pictured in Figure 2.8.

Figure 2.8. Floated layout disaster

The biggest problem with floated layouts is the need to clear the floated elements, to stop elements following a floated element from wrapping around the floated element. As our columns are now floated—removing them from the document flow—the `main div`, having no other content, has no height or width. Consequently, the background image is no longer visible and the content of the footer is wrapping around the contents of the columns as it is supposed to do, being a non-floated element. There's more detailed information about floating and clearing in the Site-Point CSS Reference.[4]

There are various methods of clearing, but one of the most simple, reliable, and commonly used methods is to put a redundant `div` element under the columns that need to be cleared. First, we add an empty `div` element with a `class` value of `clear` just before the closing tag of the `main` `div`:

```
                                                          3col-float.html (excerpt)

<div id="main">
   ⋮
  <div class="clear"> </div>
</div>
```

Next we add a CSS rule for the `clear` class:

```
                                                            3col-float.css (excerpt)

.clear {
  clear: both;
}
```

The value `both` clears all the columns, whether floated left or right. Simply clearing the footer would solve the footer problem but still leave our background missing. This method enables us to add a footer and have it sit below whichever of the three columns is the longest, as shown in Figure 2.9.

Adding bits of redundant markup isn't too much of a problem when you simply need to clear the three main columns of a layout. However, when using this technique on lots of small areas of a layout, this extra markup does add up to create a page that's larger, more complicated, and harder to maintain than what's ideal.

---

[4] http://reference.sitepoint.com/css/floatclear/

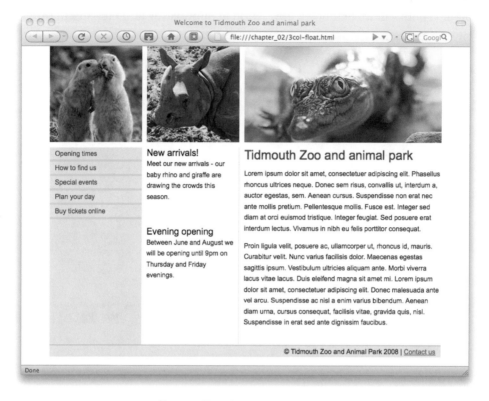

Figure 2.9. Floated layout disaster averted

For those interested in other options for clearing CSS floats without extra markup, a useful rundown of these techniques can be found on Robert Nyman's blog.[5] However, these other techniques can be complicated and have their limitations; this pragmatist has found that often the most robust method is the one outlined above—even if it does add a bit of "weight" to the page.

All this talk about clearing floats has also obscured the fact that the background image is still required to achieve a full-height column background, just as it was with the absolutely positioned layout. Also, we still require our width declaration for the main div element to make the layout work in IE6.

As we've seen, the current methods of laying out pages do have their problems. Developers can negotiate many of the problems by combining the two outlined

---

[5] http://www.robertnyman.com/2007/04/12/how-to-clear-css-floats-without-extra-markup-different-techniques-explained/

methods in one layout—perhaps by using a floated main layout, but employing positioning for internal elements. However, just to achieve the relatively simple and common layout of three columns with a footer does require a good understanding of CSS positioning and the issues involved.

It's no wonder that there's a very vocal contingent within the web design community who have maintained throughout the rise of CSS-based layout that sticking with HTML tables is the easiest way to lay out a web page—just for the luxury of being able to set a background image on a column and have it extend all of the way down the page!

What is needed is a CSS technique that provides the simplicity of grid layouts with HTML tables, without having to use table markup.

Using CSS Tables

CSS tables solve all the layout issues we've explored here regarding positioning and backgrounds in modern browsers. Specifying the value `table` for the `display` property of an element allows you to display the element and its descendants as though they're table elements. The main benefit of CSS table-based layouts is the ability to easily define the boundaries of a cell so that we can add backgrounds and so on to it—without the semantic problems of marking up non-tabular content as a HTML table in the document.

Before we dive in and discover how this works, let's create an instant demonstration. First, we make a few small changes to our markup:

3col-csstable.html (excerpt)

```
<!DOCTYPE html PUBLIC "-//W3C//DTD XHTML 1.0 Strict//EN"
    "http://www.w3.org/TR/xhtml1/DTD/xhtml1-strict.dtd">
<html xmlns="http://www.w3.org/1999/xhtml" lang="en-US">
  <head>
    ⋮ HTML head content…
  </head>
  <body>
    <div id="wrapper">
      <div id="header"></div>
      <div id="main">
        <div id="nav">
```

```
           ┊ navigation column content...
         </div>
         <div id="extras">
           ┊ news headlines column content...
         </div>
         <div id="content">
           ┊ main article content...
         </div>
       </div>
     </div>
   </body>
</html>
```

We've rearranged the HTML source so that the source order matches the content display order. The nav column comes first, followed by the extras column, and then the content column.

We also need to apply the following CSS modifications:

3col-csstable.css (excerpt)

```css
#main {
  display: table;
  border-collapse: collapse;
}
#nav {
  display: table-cell;
  width: 180px;
  background-color: #e7dbcd;
}
#extras {
  display: table-cell;
  width: 180px;
  padding-left: 10px;
  border-right: 1px dotted #d7ad7b;
}
#content {
  display: table-cell;
  width: 380px;
  padding-left: 10px;
}
```

The fresh CSS table-based layout that we've just created will display correctly in Internet Explorer 8 as well as in Firefox, Safari, and Opera; Figure 2.10 shows how it looks in IE8.

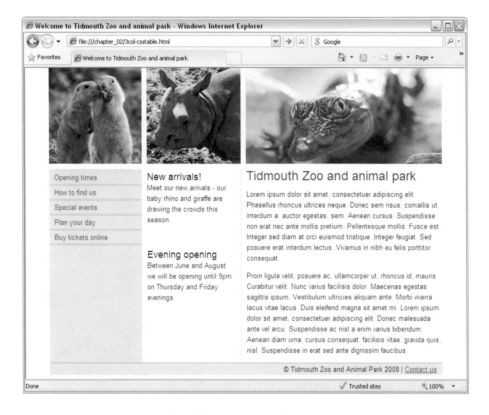

Figure 2.10. The CSS table-based layout in Internet Explorer 8

Our three-column equal-height layout is achieved without having to resort to tricks like faux columns using background images, worrying about positioning, or having to clear floats—revolutionary!

How Does This Work?

The `display` property allows you to specify a range of table-related values in order to make elements display as though they were table elements. The available `display` values are:

`table`   makes the element behave like a `table` element

table-row	makes the element behave like a table row (tr) element
table-cell	makes the element behave like a table cell (td) element
table-row-group	makes the element behave like a table body row group (tbody) element
table-header-group	makes the element behave like a table header row group (thead) element
table-footer-group	makes the element behave like a table footer row group (tfoot) element
table-caption	makes the element behave like a table caption element
table-column	makes the element behave like a table column (col) element
table-column-group	makes the element behave like a table column group (colgroup) element

 ## Hang on ... Aren't Tables for Layout Wrong?

Perhaps you're feeling slightly uncomfortable about the example we've just seen—after all, haven't web standards advocates like myself been insisting for years that you shouldn't be using tables for layout?

The table element in HTML is a semantic structure: it describes *what data is*. Therefore, you should only use the table element if the data you are marking up is tabular—for example, a table of financial information. If it would normally be stored in a spreadsheet on your computer, it probably needs marking up as a table in HTML.

The table value of the display property, on the other hand, is simply an indication of how something should look in the browser—it has no semantic meaning. Using a table element for your layout tells a user-agent, "This data is tabular." Using a bunch of divs that have the display property set to table and table-cell says nothing to that user-agent other than asking it to render them visually in a certain way, if it's capable of doing so.

> Of course, we should also take care not to use `display: table;` on a bunch of `div` elements when what we *really* have is tabular data!

Our simple example above makes our layout behave as if it were a single row table with three cells; it doesn't take much imagination to realize the potential of this technique for creating complex grid layouts with ease.

Anonymous Table Elements

CSS tables happily abide by the normal rules of table layout, which enables an extremely powerful feature of CSS table layouts: missing table elements are created anonymously by the browser. The CSS2.1 specification states:[6]

> Document languages other than HTML may not contain all the elements in the CSS 2.1 table model. In these cases, the "missing" elements must be assumed in order for the table model to work. Any table element will automatically generate necessary anonymous table objects around itself, consisting of at least three nested objects corresponding to a "table"/"inline-table" element, a "table-row" element, and a "table-cell" element.

What this means is that if we use `display: table-cell;` without first containing the cell in a block set to `display: table-row;`, the row will be implied—the browser will act as though the declared row is actually there.

Let's use a simple example to investigate this feature: the three-cell grid layout shown in Figure 2.11. We'll look at three different HTML markup samples that will result in the same visual layout.

---

[6] http://www.w3.org/TR/CSS21/tables.html#anonymous-boxes

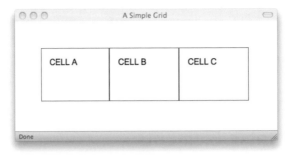

Figure 2.11. A simple grid layout

First, here's a sample of markup that can be used to generate the three-cell layout:

```
<div class="container">
  <div class="row">
    <div class="cell">CELL A</div>
    <div class="cell">CELL B</div>
    <div class="cell">CELL C</div>
  </div>
</div>
```

A set of nested div elements may not seem so very exciting, but hang in there, we're building to something. The CSS is also very simple:

```
.container {
  display: table;
}
.row {
  display: table-row;
}
.cell {
  display: table-cell;
  width: 100px;
  height: 100px;
  border: 1px solid blue;
  padding: 1em;
}
```

The CSS above sets the element with a class of container to display: table, an element with a class of row to display: table-row, and an element with a class of `cell` to `display: table-cell`, as well as giving it a `border` and a `height` and `width`.

This HTML markup above explicitly creates elements for the table and row surrounding the three cells, using all of the CSS classes that we've created. However, we can reduce the markup, removing the `row` div element like so:

```
<div class="row">
  <div class="cell">CELL A</div>
  <div class="cell">CELL B</div>
  <div class="cell">CELL C</div>
</div>
```

Even though the above markup is missing the element representing the table row, the row will be created by the browser as an anonymous box. We can reduce the markup even further:

```
<div class="cell">CELL A</div>
<div class="cell">CELL B</div>
<div class="cell">CELL C</div>
```

The above markup is missing the elements representing the table row and the table; these are both created as anonymous boxes by the browser. Even with the elements missing in markup, the end product, shown in Figure 2.11, is the same.

Rules for the Creation of Anonymous Table Elements

These anonymous boxes are not created by magic, and they won't automatically make up for any deficiencies in your HTML code. To be able to take full advantage of anonymous table elements, you'd best become familiar with the rules for their creation. If a layout calls for an implied element, the browser will create an anonymous box and set its CSS `display` property to one of `table`, `table-row`, or `table-cell`, depending on the context.

If you have an element that has been set to `display: table-cell;` but its immediate parent (the containing element) is not set to `table-row`, an anonymous box set to `table-row` will be created to enclose the cell and any subsequent adjacent sibling elements that are also set to `table-cell`, until it encounters an element not set to table-cell, so they'll all end up in the same row. This is the case with the following markup:

```
<div class="cell">CELL A</div>
<div class="cell">CELL B</div>
<div class="cell">CELL C</div>
<div>Not a cell</div>
```

The three div elements above that have a class of cell are set to display: table-cell; and will appear side by side as though they're in a single row table; the last div element won't be included in the row, because it isn't set to display: table-cell;.

If an element is set to display: table-row; while its parent element isn't set to table (or table-row-group), an anonymous box set to display: table; will be created to enclose the row, and any subsequent adjacent sibling elements will be set to display: table-row. Also, if the element with display set to table-row lacks an element set to table-cell directly within it, an anonymous box set to table-cell will be created to enclose all the elements within the table-row element. Consider the following markup:

```
<div class="row">ROW A</div>
<div class="row">ROW B</div>
<div>Not a row</div>
```

The two div elements above with a class of row are set to display: table-row; and will appear one under the other as though they're rows in the same single-column table. The last div element won't be included in the implied table.

Similarly, if an element is set to any of the other display values that match elements which would naturally exist directly inside a parent table element such as table-row-group, table-header-group, table-footer-group, table-column, table-column-group, and table-caption, but does not have a parent set to display: table;, an anonymous box set to table will be created to enclose the element and any subsequent adjacent sibling elements with suitable display values.

Other Useful Table Properties

When using CSS tables, because the elements conform to the normal rules for table layout, you can also apply other table-related CSS properties. Here's a few that can come in handy:

table-layout

Setting the `table-layout` to `fixed` tells the browser that the table should render with the fixed algorithm for formatting the cell widths. This is useful in a fixed-width layout, such as the one we created earlier.[7]

border-collapse

Just as with regular HTML tables, you can use the `border-collapse` property to specify that your table layout elements use collapsed (with the value `collapse`) or separated (with the value `separate`) borders between the cell elements.

border-spacing

If you specify the value `separate` for the `border-collapse` property, you can then use the `border-spacing` property to specify the width of the space between the cell element borders.

Making a Perfect Grid

Making a grid of equal height elements has always been a challenge using traditional CSS layout techniques, but it's something to which CSS tables are well suited. For example, if we want to create an image gallery comprising a grid of images with captions, such as the one shown in Figure 2.12, using a CSS table renders the task simple.

---

[7] You can read more about how the table layout algorithms work in the SitePoint CSS reference, available at http://reference.sitepoint.com/css/tableformatting.

Figure 2.12. The gallery grid demo in Internet Explorer 8

The markup for our gallery is as follows:

```
                                        csstable-grid.html (excerpt)

<div class="grid">
  <div class="row">
    <div class="image">
      <img src="images/photo1.jpg" alt="A Lily" />
      <p>A lily in the gardens of The Vyne Country House</p>
    </div>
    <div class="image">
      <img src="images/photo3.jpg" alt="A Fuchsia plant" />
      <p>Fuchsia plant in my garden</p>
    </div>
  </div>
  <div class="row">
    <div class="image">
```

```
      <img src="images/photo2.jpg"
          alt="A crazy looking Allium flower" />
      <p>A crazy looking flower</p>
    </div>
    <div class="image">
      <img src="images/photo4.jpg"
          alt="A Robin sitting on a fence" />
      <p>This robin has been visiting our garden over the summer.
          He is very friendly and doesn't seem to be too worried
          about sharing the garden with us.</p>
    </div>
  </div>
</div>
```

Each gallery image cell is comprised of an img element and a caption in a p element contained within a div element with a class of image. Each row is contained within a div element within a class of row, and the whole gallery is contained within a div with a class of grid.

The CSS required to lay out our grid is simple:

csstable-grid.css *(excerpt)*

```
.grid {
  display: table;
  border-spacing: 4px;
}
.row {
  display: table-row;
}
.image {
  display: table-cell;
  width: 240px;
  background-color: #000;
  border: 8px solid #000;
  vertical-align: top;
  text-align: center;
}
.image p {
  color: #fff;
  font-size: 85%;
```

```
    text-align: left;
    padding-top: 8px;
}
```

The above CSS is fairly straightforward, but you might notice how we've made use of the `border-spacing` property to control the spacing of our gallery image cells. Making a grid layout couldn't be easier—and we've avoided any headaches over equal heights or fragile layouts made with floated elements.

Essentially, most of what we do with CSS layout nowadays is a total hack. We're using floats, and absolute positioning, and negative margins, and any other tricks we happen to stumble upon to produce basic designs. Designs that have been essential to visual design for as long as designers can remember—columns, sidebars, pullquotes. Basic layout. Lining this up with that.

Even though the use of HTML tables for layout was a shortsighted and misguided move, it did match the way that we lay out our pages more logically. And, visually, they are a better match for the layout of pages than using a bunch of nested floats. The only problem is, they're evil. *That's* why I can't wait to use CSS table layout for laying out content. Because it's not a hack. Because it does what we want in a logical way; in a way that it was intended for us to use.

Taking a look at the CSS I employed to lay out forms in a consistent manner, I could have avoided a whole bunch of headaches if CSS table layout was available. The rigid structure of forms—titles, columns, fields—is a perfect match for a grid structure—a table structure—so why can't we lay it out in a table-like manner? I know that many people have succumbed to using HTML tables out of the frustrations involved in wrangling the CSS for a form. So I, for one, can't wait to see how CSS table layout will transform the way we approach page layout on the Web.

—Cameron Adams[8]

---

[8] http://www.themaninblue.com/

Putting Principles into Practice

This chapter has presented a basic primer to the usage of the table-related values of the CSS `display` property—finally, a source of relief for all those struggling to construct reliable grid-based layouts using CSS! We began by examining the current layout options of absolute positioning and floated elements, and the many issues to consider when implementing them. We then had an introduction to the straightforward approach to layout provided by CSS tables. We explored the various table-related `display` values available, looked at the nature of anonymous table elements, and discovered some other useful CSS table properties.

The next step is up to you—with any luck, you have realized the potential CSS tables provide for creating grid layouts, and are now bursting with curiosity! Using the knowledge gained in this chapter, you're all set up to begin experimenting with your own CSS table layouts and create new techniques.

Now, we'll move on to consider some of the most common questions about CSS table layouts in the next chapter, and provide concrete solutions.

Chapter 3

CSS Table Solutions

As we've seen in the previous chapter, using table display properties offers a whole new bag of tricks to the designer. This approach can simplify CSS layout and allow exciting new opportunities. If questions are now springing into your mind, this chapter will help to provide some answers and help you on your way to understanding the potential of CSS table layouts.

Can CSS tables be used to create flexible layouts?

The examples we've seen so far have been concerned with fixed-width layouts. We can also use CSS tables to create the flexible layouts—columns that resize to the width of the user's screen—often referred to as **liquid layouts**.

If we set the containing div to 100%, the table will take up the whole width of the parent—in the case of a liquid layout, the parent will be the viewport. In a multi-column layout, we can then set our side columns to have either a fixed width in pixels, ems, or a percentage width, but leave the main column without a specified width so that it expands to fill the rest of the space.

A few simple changes can turn our fixed-width layout into a liquid layout with two fixed sidebars and a variable-width main content area:

3col-csstable-liquid.css *(excerpt)*

```
#wrapper {
  ⋮
  width: 100%;
}
#header {
  height: 180px;
  background-image: url(images/header.jpg);
  background-repeat: no-repeat;
  margin-bottom: 10px;
  background-color: #d5b87e;
}
#main {
  display: table;
  border-collapse: collapse;
  width: 100%;
}
#content {
  display: table-cell;
  padding: 0 50px 0 10px;
}
```

This exercise will create the liquid three-column layout shown in Figure 3.1. To achieve the main structure of this layout, I simply set the wrapper div element to 100%, the width for the main div element to 100%, and removed the width property on the content cell—everything else was just tweaking to improve the page's appearance as its width became variable.

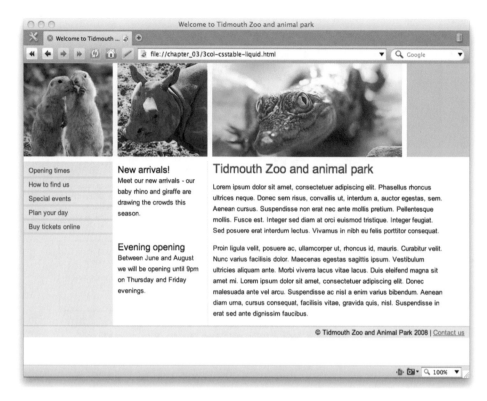

Figure 3.1. A liquid three-column CSS table layout in Opera 9.5

Can CSS tables be nested?

Table display with CSS isn't only useful for complete page layouts; it can also help with the layout of smaller elements within larger layouts. Let's take a look at an example of nesting a CSS table.

We now want to convert the `extras` column into a promotional box in the middle of the content area, to achieve the result shown in Figure 3.2.

Figure 3.2. Nested CSS tables in Safari 3.1

We *could* attempt to do this with floated elements. However, using floats to create a two-column box with borders and matching column heights is tricky. With CSS tables, though, this task is as simple as it ought to be!

I've removed the middle `extras` column from the markup and increased the width of the `content` area in our CSS, in order to convert it to a two-column layout. Here's the markup for the new `promo` block:

nested-csstable.html *(excerpt)*

```html
<div class="promo">
  <div class="arrivals">
    <h3>New arrivals!</h3>
    <p>Meet our new arrivals - our baby rhino and giraffe are
        drawing the crowds this season.</p>
  </div>
  <div class="news">
    <h3>Latest news</h3>
    <ul>
      <li>Sed nec erat sed sem molestie congue.
          Cras lacus sapien, <a href="http://www.example.com">
          ultrices ac…</a></li>
      <li>Aliquam egestas arcu a massa. In hendrerit
          <a href="http://www.example.com">
          odio eget lectus…</a></li>
    </ul>
  </div>
</div>
```

With the above markup added to the source within the main column, all we need to do is apply the following CSS:

nested-csstable.css *(excerpt)*

```css
.promo {
  display: table;
  width: 560px;
  border: 2px solid #5a3811;
  border-collapse: collapse;
  margin-bottom: 1em;
}
.promo .arrivals {
  width: 160px;
  display: table-cell;
  border: 2px solid #5a3811;
  padding: 10px;
  background-color: #e7dbcd;
}
```

```
.promo .news {
  width: 340px;
  display: table-cell;
  border: 2px solid #5a3811;
  padding: 10px;
}
.promo h3 {
  font-size: 110%;
  font-weight: normal;
  color: #5a3811;
}
.promo ul {
  list-style: none;
}
.promo p, .promo li {
  font-size: 75%;
}
```

This small two-column box works in exactly the same way as the main layout. We set the promo div element to display: table; and the two div containers, news and arrivals, to display: table-cell;. We're then free to add any borders and background colors that we like.

That's all there is to it! We've achieved a two-column promotional nested block element without having to worry about creating pretend equal-height columns using background images, or clearing floats.

How can I position elements within a table cell?

A common practice when dealing with positioning within a block element is to create a new **positioning context** by setting the position property of the block element to relative. This allows us to position elements within the block, relative to its top, right, bottom, or left.

However, when setting position: relative; on an element that also has a table-related display value specified, the positioning is ignored. This behavior has previously been documented by Alastair Campbell,[1] who points out in his article that the CSS 2.1 spec is not clear on what browsers should do when an element displaying as a table element is relatively positioned:[2]

> The effect of `position: relative` on `table-row-group`, `table-header-group`, `table-footer-group`, `table-row`, `table-column-group`, `table-column`, `table-cell`, and `table-caption` elements *is undefined*.

This behavior is, in my opinion, the biggest problem with using CSS tables for layout. Let's say, for example, that we position an "**All news items**" link at the bottom-right corner of the promo box that we developed in the section called "Can CSS tables be nested?", as depicted in Figure 3.3.

Figure 3.3. Correctly positioned "**All news items**" link

In this situation, I would commonly add `position: relative` to the containing box in order to create a new positioning context, and then use absolute positioning to place the link in the bottom-right corner. However, in the case of CSS tables, the containing element is one that displays as a table cell and the relative positioning has no effect; it doesn't create the required positioning context.

---

[1] http://alastairc.ac/2006/06/css-tables-verses-layout-tables/
[2] http://www.w3.org/TR/CSS21/visuren.html#positioning-scheme

Here's the markup for our promotions box with the added "**All news items**" link:

```
                                      csstable-position-01.html (excerpt)

<div class="promo">
  <div class="arrivals">
    <h1>New arrivals!</h1>
    <p>Meet our new arrivals - our baby rhino and giraffe are
        drawing the crowds this season.</p>
  </div>
  <div class="news">
    <h1>Latest news</h1>
    <ul>
      <li>Sed nec erat sed sem molestie congue.
          Cras lacus sapien, <a href="http://www.example.com">
          ultrices ac...</a></li>
      <li>Aliquam egestas arcu a massa. In hendrerit
          <a href="http://www.example.com">
          odio eget lectus...</a></li>
      <li id="allnewslink"><a href="http://www.example.com">
                All news items</a></li>
    </ul>
  </div>
</div>
```

Our CSS hasn't changed much since the section called "Can CSS tables be nested?", the only difference being that we've added a rule for the new link:

```
                                       csstable-position-01.css (excerpt)

#allnewslink {
  position: absolute;
  bottom: 0;
  right: 0;
  padding: 0;
}
```

Predictably, our new link appears at the bottom-right of the viewport as shown in Figure 3.4. If the positioning context is not provided by the containing block element, our absolutely positioned link will either be:

- positioned at the bottom right of the nearest positioned ancestor element—the next parent, or the parent's parent (and so on) of the containing block that has `position` set to `absolute` or `relative`

- positioned at the bottom right of the viewport

There's no straightforward approach to fixing this problem using CSS tables, but we can take one of two simple approaches to provide a positioning context: add a positioned child block element to the cell, or wrap the table in a positioned element.

Figure 3.4. The link is positioned relative to the viewport and not the cell

To be able to add a child block element, we must be able to specify the `height` and `width` of the element. Let's first add the child element to our markup:

csstable-position-02.html *(excerpt)*

```
<div class="promo">
  <div class="arrivals">
    <h1>New arrivals!</h1>
    <p>Meet our new arrivals - our baby rhino and giraffe are
        drawing the crowds this season.</p>
  </div>
  <div class="news">
    <div class="news-inner">
      <h1>Latest news</h1>
      <ul>
        <li>Sed nec erat sed sem molestie congue.
            Cras lacus sapien, <a href="http://www.example.com">
```

```
            ultrices ac...</a></li>
        <li>Aliquam egestas arcu a massa. In hendrerit
            <a href="http://www.example.com">
            odio eget lectus...</a></li>
        <li id="allnewslink"><a href="http://www.example.com">
            All news items</a></li>
      </ul>
    </div>
  </div>
</div>
```

A small modification to our CSS and the position of the link is corrected:

csstable-position-02.css *(excerpt)*

```
.promo .news {
  width: 340px;
  height: 125px;
  display: table-cell;
  border: 2px solid #5a3811;
}
.promo .news-inner {
  position: relative;
  width: 340px;
  height: 125px;
  padding: 10px;
}
```

In the above CSS, we've had to do a little tweaking. We created a new rule for the news-inner div element with the all-important position: relative; declaration, specified a height and width matching the height and width of the cell, and moved the padding declaration from the cell element to the new child element. The result is the one depicted previously in Figure 3.3.

Since we've been able to specify a height for the inner child element, we can position the link at the bottom of the cell, but what if we can't predict how many news items will appear in that list on any given day? If we can't predict the height of the element, we can make a slight adjustment to the CSS:

```
                                    csstable-position-02.css (excerpt)
.promo .news-inner {
  position: relative;
  width: 340px;
  min-height: 125px;
  padding: 10px;
}
```

Instead of specifying a height, we've changed the property to min-height. This change will allow the height of the cell to grow and maintain the position of the link.

To support a flexible-height table, we can also try another approach: wrapping the table. Let's change the markup in such a way that the whole layout is wrapped in a block element (and add a few more news items while we're at it):

```
                                    csstable-position-03.html (excerpt)
<div class="promo-outer">
  <div class="promo">
    <div class="arrivals">
      <h1>New arrivals!</h1>
      <p>Meet our new arrivals - our baby rhino and giraffe are
          drawing the crowds this season.</p>
    </div>
    <div class="news">
      <h1>Latest news</h1>
      <ul>
        ⋮ existing news items…
        <li>Sed nec erat sed sem molestie congue.
            Cras lacus sapien, <a href="http://www.example.com">
            ultrices ac...</a></li>
        <li>Aliquam egestas arcu a massa. In hendrerit
            <a href="http://www.example.com">
            odio eget lectus...</a></li>
        <li id="allnewslink"><a href="http://www.example.com">
            All news items</a></li>
      </ul>
    </div>
  </div>
</div>
```

If we set the width of the promo-outer div element correctly, we'll be able to use it as the positioning element for our link. Here are the changes to the CSS:

```css
.promo-outer {
  position: relative;
  width: 560px;
}
.promo .news {
  width: 340px;
  display: table-cell;
  border: 2px solid #5a3811;
  padding: 10px 10px 20px 10px;
}
#allnewslink {
  position: absolute;
  bottom: 2px;
  right: 12px;
  padding: 0;
}
```

Once again, all we've had to do is a little tweaking. We set the outer element width, adjusted the padding of the news cell to allow some additional bottom padding to provide space for the link, and adjusted the position of the link (making an allowance for the two-pixel border on the cell). Thus our desired layout is achieved, no matter how many news items appear in the list, as we can see in Figure 3.5.

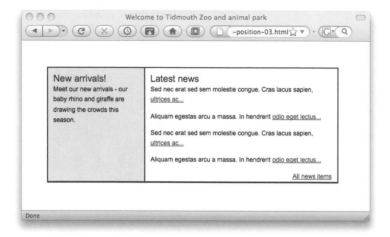

Figure 3.5. Flexible positioning for the **"All news items"** link

You've probably realized that both of the above approaches are situation-specific—they're not generic solutions. The lack of an available positioning context in elements that have a table-related `display` value is a significant problem, which will need to be solved on a case-by-case basis if it arises in your layouts.

Do CSS tables support the `colspan` and `rowspan` attributes?

If you've had experience building layouts using HTML tables, you'll be familiar with the use of the `colspan` and `rowspan` attributes of the `td` element. These attributes offer complex possibilities to a simple table, enabling cells to span columns and rows.

CSS tables lack any concept of row or column spanning, making it trickier to use one single layout structure than what might have been possible when using HTML tables. However, similar layouts can be achieved by using nested CSS tables.

In this example, we use nested tables to simulate a three-column layout where the two outer columns appear to span both rows of the table. Look at the markup; you can see that the layout is basically a three-column table layout with a second table nested within the middle column:

csstable-nested-layout.html *(excerpt)*

```
<div id="nav">LEFT</div>
<div id="content">
  <div class="row">
    <div class="inner-content">A</div>
    <div class="inner-content">B</div>
  </div>
  <div class="row">
    <div class="inner-content">C</div>
    <div class="inner-content">D</div>
  </div>
</div>
<div id="extras">RIGHT</div>
```

To transform the div elements in the above markup into columns, with the addition of some padding and borders for clarity, we apply the following CSS:

csstable-nested-layout.css *(excerpt)*

```
#nav, #extras {
  display: table-cell;
  width: 100px;
  padding: 1em;
  border: 1px solid red;
}
#content {
  display: table-cell;
  padding: 1em;
  border: 1px solid red;
}
.row {
  display: table-row;
}
.inner-content {
  display: table-cell;
  width: 100px;
  height: 100px;
  padding: 1em;
  border: 1px dashed #666;
}
```

The nav, content, and extras div elements become cells in the outer table; the div elements with the class row become the rows of the inner table in the middle column. The result is pictured in Figure 3.6.

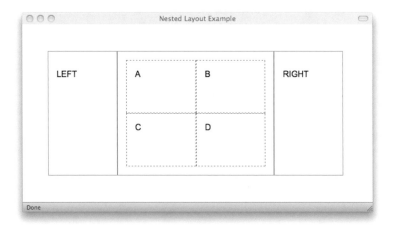

Figure 3.6. Nested CSS tables

Also, you may have noticed how we took advantage of anonymous table elements in the example above—there's no element displaying as a table element for the inner or outer table. We've been able to make use of anonymous table elements as we've specified the widths of the cells. If we wanted a full-width table, however, we'd have to add an element with display: table;, so that we could then apply a width of 100%; we can't specify any CSS for anonymous elements.

It's also possible to simulate row and column spanning using absolute positioning of table cells in many cases. In this example, we'll make the second cell of the first row of a table span both rows of the table (as if it had a rowspan of 2). First, let's take a look at the HTML code:

csstable-rowspan.html (excerpt)

```
<div class="tablewrapper">
  <div class="table">
    <div class="row">
      <div class="cell">
        Top left
      </div>
      <div class="rowspanned cell">
```

```
      Center
    </div>
    <div class="cell">
      Top right
    </div>
  </div>
  <div class="row">
    <div class="cell">
      Bottom left
    </div>
    <div class="empty cell"></div>
    <div class="cell">
      Bottom right
    </div>
  </div>
  </div>
</div>
```

You'll notice that we've wrapped our table div in an extra div with a class of tablewrapper. This extra div is needed to provide a CSS positioning context—which we create by giving it relative positioning:

csstable-rowspan.css *(excerpt)*

```
.tablewrapper {
  position: relative;
}
```

According to the CSS spec, we should be able to simply apply relative positioning to the table div, but current browsers don't seem to support this.

Now, we can use absolute positioning to control the size and position of the div with class rowspanned cell:

csstable-rowspan.css *(excerpt)*

```
.cell.rowspanned {
  position: absolute;
  top: 0;
  bottom: 0;
  width: 100px;
}
```

With the `top` and `bottom` properties both set to zero, the cell will stretch to fill the full height of the table, simulating a row span. Depending on the needs of your layout, you could use different values for `top` and `bottom`, or even set the cell's `height` directly to achieve other row-spanning layouts.

You also need to specify the width of the cell. Usually, the easiest way to do this is just to set its `width` property, but depending what you know of the dimensions of surrounding table cells, you could also do this by setting `left` and `right`.

Since the positioned cell doesn't *actually* span multiple rows of the table, the table must still contain a corresponding cell in each of the other rows. These cells are simply empty placeholders, though; note the `div` with `class empty cell` in the HTML code above. The function of this cell is to hold open the space that will be occupied by the "spanned" cell, so we must ensure its width matches the width we specified for the `rowspanned cell`:

```
.cell.empty {
  width: 100px;
}
```

And that's all there is to it! To complete the style sheet for this example, we need only set the appropriate `display` property values, and add some borders so we can see what's going on:

csstable-rowspan.css (excerpt)

```
.tablewrapper {
  position: relative;
}
.table {
  display: table;
}
.row {
  display: table-row;
}
.cell {
  border: 1px solid red;
  display: table-cell;
}
.cell.empty
```

```
{
  border: none;
  width: 100px;
}
.cell.rowspanned {
  position: absolute;
  top: 0;
  bottom: 0;
  width: 100px;
}
```

In essence, by using absolute positioning we are telling the browser, "Let me handle the layout of this table cell—you take care of the rest." The results can be seen in Figure 3.7.

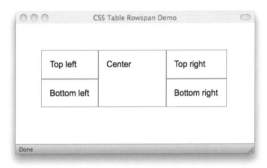

Figure 3.7. A cell with a simulated rowspan

What's going wrong with these anonymous table elements?

While anonymous table elements can be useful, they can also cause frustration—after all, we have no control over them. Anonymous elements are predictable most of the time, but you may find your expectations are not met and your layout is disrupted. For example, the browser might create an anonymous cell rather than the row you were expecting.

If you're having trouble getting your page layout to behave, you might like to play it safe and create actual elements in place of anonymous elements. If we want to play it safe with our Tidmouth Zoo layout, we add the `div` element that will act as the table row:

```
<body>
  <div id="wrapper">
    <div id="header"></div>
    <div id="main">
      <div class="inner">
        <div id="nav">
            ⋮ navigation column content…
        </div>
        <div id="extras">
          ⋮ news headlines column content…
        </div>
        <div id="content">
          ⋮ main article content…
        </div>
      </div>
    </div>
  </div>
</body>
```

We then need to add one more rule to our CSS:

```
#main .inner {
  display: table-row;
}
```

Anonymous Elements in Firefox

A long-standing bug in Firefox[3] that affects the creation of anonymous boxes can mean that, in some circumstances, your display doesn't load as expected, and can also cause problems if you want to modify elements using JavaScript. You may find that your layout loads with one column dropped below the others, but will snap into position when you refresh the page. If this is the case, you may have to add an actual element with `display` set to `table-row` or `table-row-group` where an element would otherwise be implied.

---

[3] https://bugzilla.mozilla.org/show_bug.cgi?id=148810

Another way that anonymous tabled elements might be confusing is if you have a different number of cell elements in each row. Tables, of course, require the same number of cells in each row; if not, the browser will attempt to display the table as best it can; often a less than optimal result.

Consider the following markup for a simple three-row grid as an example:

```
<div id="head">TOP</div>
<div id="content">
  <div class="cell">A</div>
  <div class="cell">B</div>
  <div class="cell">C</div>
</div>
<div id="foot">BOTTOM</div>
```

We apply the following CSS to the above markup:

```
#head, #content, #foot {
  display: table-row;
  background-color: #ccc;
}
.cell {
  display: table-cell;
  width: 100px;
  height: 100px;
  border: 1px dashed #000;
  padding: 1em;
}
```

Our intention is to create a three-row display with three columns within the middle row, but the result is something completely different, as Figure 3.8 shows.

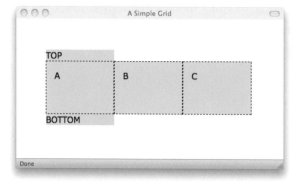

Figure 3.8. A problem with anonymous table elements

According to the section called "Rules for the Creation of Anonymous Table Elements" in Chapter 2, if a row element has no child elements set to display as a table cell, a single anonymous cell element will be created to contain all of the contents of the row element. This means that our table has a single cell in the top and bottom row, but three cells in between.

One possible solution is to add another element to the middle row to encompass the three cells in that row and act as a nested table, like so:

```
<div id="head">TOP</div>
<div id="content">
  <div class="content-wrap">
    <div class="cell">A</div>
    <div class="cell">B</div>
    <div class="cell">C</div>
  </div>
</div>
<div id="foot">BOTTOM</div>
```

We then need to apply the following CSS:

```
.content-wrap {
  display: table;
}
```

The result of our changes can be seen in Figure 3.9. There are many other ways to change the markup in order to provide enough layout context so that the browser can display your layout as you intended, but I'll leave it up to your experimentation!

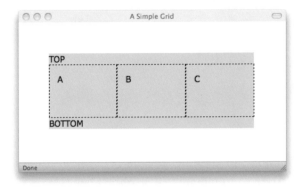

Figure 3.9. Our layout is fixed

Making use of anonymous table elements is a great way to reduce the amount of markup required for your layout—but make sure to test it to ensure that the anonymous elements are being created as you expect.

Do I have to change the source order?

If you're arranging columns, your source order needs to match the order in which you want your columns displayed. Our original three-column layout from Chapter 2 required us to move the `nav` and `extras div` elements before the `content div` in the source, so that the columns would display in that order.

However, there is a situation where we can take advantage of the nature of table layout and still be able to control the source order of your content. If your site places navigation and other elements at the top of the page layout, and a footer at the bottom of the page layout, you can make use of the `display` property values `table-header-group` and `table-footer-group`.

For example, consider the following hypothetical markup:

```
<div id="content">
  <div id="article-body">
    : main page article body content…
```

```
      </div>
      <div id="article-supporting-info">
        ⋮ article supporting content…
      </div>
    </div>
    <div id="article-footer">
      ⋮ article footer content…
    </div>
    <div id="navigation">
      ⋮ web site navigation links…
    </div>
```

Our article content appears first in the source, followed by the article footer, and then the site navigation. To make the navigation display above the article content when our page is viewed in a browser, all we have to do is apply this CSS:

```
#content {
  display: table-row-group;
}
#article-body {
  display:table-cell;
}
#article-supporting-info {
  display:table-cell;
}
#footer {
  display:table-footer-group;
}
#navigation {
  display:table-header-group;
}
```

By treating the navigation div element as the table header, the content div as the table body, and the footer div as the table footer, the browser will display the elements in the order that we want. Some work will still be required within those main structural elements—you may need nested CSS tables—but this solution is useful if it suits your desired layout.

Is the source order really a problem?

Much of the debate since the beginnings of CSS layout has been concerned with the subject of source order. The ability to order the source of your document in a way that presents the main content before navigation and secondary content is widely regarded to be beneficial in two main areas: search engine optimization (SEO) and accessibility.

In terms of SEO, it's often thought that putting your most important keyword-rich content near the top of the document in the source will help it to be ranked higher for those keywords. Regarding accessibility, a commonly held assumption is that if a person is navigating your site using a screen reader and you have a large menu that's the same at the top of each page, it will be beneficial to organize the source in such a way that the content is always the first area reached by a screen reader user.

The truth is, however, that source order has little impact on either of those areas. Of far more importance than source order is a proper heading structure: a properly nested sequence of heading tags (<h1> to <h6>) to clearly identify the page topic and sections.

Heading tags are automatically discovered and prioritized by search engines. A well thought-out heading structure will allow your page content to be properly indexed.

Research presented by Roger Hudson, Russ Weakley, and Lisa Miller at the OZeWAI Conference on 9th December, 2005, concluded that "the source order of a web page is likely to be of little relevance to the majority of screen reader users."[4] In addition, it confirmed the importance of structural labels and advocated the provision of **skip links**—simple links at the top of a document that allow the user to jump to the main content area, offering the choice of whether to go through the menu or to hop over it. The official web site of the Web Standards Project[5] uses skip links to great effect; you can see one at the top of the screen pictured in Figure 3.10.

---

[4] http://usability.com.au/resources/source-order.cfm
[5] http://www.webstandards.org/

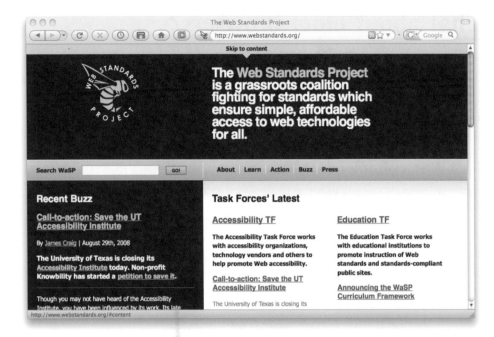

Figure 3.10. **Skip to content** link on the Web Standards Project web site

Witnessing the browser market shift, it's exciting to see new ways to approach how we code a design. Over the years, we've seen some creative ways to pull off the effects that we've wanted, like columnar layouts. Float-based designs, faux columns, absolute positioning: they've all just been tricks. They're illusions compared to what old-style tables gave us. Thankfully, CSS table properties give us true columns while maintaining the flexibility that CSS gives us and the semantics that HTML offers.

Even though browsers like Firefox have supported them for years, we've been unable to truly take advantage of them because of that elephant in the room: Internet Explorer. Luckily, IE8 will finally give us what we've wanted and maybe we'll see some ingenious designs made possible that would not have been possible before.

—Jonathan Snook[6]

---

[6] http://snook.ca/jonathan/

What about older browsers?

Well, I'm glad you asked! In this chapter, we've addressed the most common questions about CSS tables and looked at some of the ways they can make CSS layouts easier to achieve. But, of course, there's still the problem of what to do about Internet Explorer 6 and 7; it's an inescapable fact that, together, they represent a majority of the browsers in use today.

Answering this question is the focus of the next chapter, where we'll look at how we can address the needs of older browsers that do not support CSS tables.

Considering Older Browsers

So far, we've discovered how CSS tables can simplify both CSS layout and enable effects such as full-height columns, which we're currently obliged to fake via fragile and problematic hacks. Wouldn't it be nice if, all of a sudden, you could stop using those hacks and simply rely on CSS tables for all your layout work? Fantastic, you say, but of course this can only be a utopian vision—Internet Explorer 6 and 7, as the two major browser versions currently in use that do not support CSS tables, make this dream impossible.

But the release of Internet Explorer 8, with full support for CSS tables, will change all this. Exactly how it'll change *your* life is the subject we'll explore in this chapter. As we'll see, it is our responsibility as web professionals to go as far as we possibly can in adopting these new CSS techniques, even if it means sacrificing some degree of design fidelity in older browsers.

Support for CSS Tables

Table 4.1 shows current versions of browsers and their support for CSS tables. Aside from Internet Explorer 8, which has not been released at the time of writing, I've taken the list of browsers from the Yahoo Graded Browser Support list of A-Grade browsers.[1] These are the browsers that Yahoo has identified as covering 96% of its users, and should be given full support in web design.

You, the Browser Support Matrix, and Your Clients

The Yahoo Graded Browser Support matrix is a great way to show clients the range of browsers that are in use and that are worth investing time to support. Supporting very old browsers fully—trying to give someone using Internet Explorer 5, for example, the same experience as someone using Internet Explorer 7—can limit the design choices you can make, as well as being time-consuming and expensive. Being able to point to the list that Yahoo uses to decide which browsers to fully support can be very useful indeed. Remember to emphasize that Yahoo is *not* locking out users of older browsers, but simply giving them a pared-down experience.

Table 4.1. Chart showing support for CSS tables

Browser	Support
Firefox 3	Supported
Firefox 2	Supported
IE 8.0	Supported
IE 7.0	No Support
IE 6.0	No Support
Opera 9.5	Supported
Safari 3	Supported

As you can see from this table, most browsers in common use have support for CSS tables—unfortunately, the two browsers that do not, namely Internet Explorer 6 and 7, are still widely used.

How to deal with these two stragglers once Internet Explorer 8 hits the streets is a question every web designer will have to answer on a project-by-project basis. It's also a question that we have faced before.

---

[1] http://developer.yahoo.com/yui/articles/gbs/

To Hell with Bad Browsers

In 2001, Jeffrey Zeldman, then leader of the Web Standards Project,[2] published a groundbreaking article on the A List Apart site: *To Hell With Bad Browsers.*[3] This manifesto was to change the face of the Web for many of us authoring sites at the time. Zeldman wrote:

> For years, the goal of a Web that was accessible to all looked more like an opium dream than reality. Then, in the year 2000, Microsoft, Netscape, and Opera began delivering the goods. At last we can repay their efforts by using these standards in our sites. We encourage others to do the same.

The burden of moving the Web forward had shifted away from browser makers and onto browser users and web designers. For progress to be made, users would have to upgrade to newer browsers and designers would have to begin using the features of those new browsers.

To encourage this direction, WaSP launched the Browser Upgrade Campaign, shown in Figure 4.1, at the same time that Zeldman's manifesto was published. The campaign advocated using one of two methods to let users know they should upgrade their browsers. The "gentle" method involved displaying your page without style information for users of old browsers such as Netscape 4, adding a suggestion at the top of the page that users consider upgrading their browsers. The alternate method was to actually block users of old browsers from accessing the site, redirecting them to a browser upgrade message—either on your own site or on the WaSP web site.

---

[2] http://webstandards.org/
[3] http://www.alistapart.com/stories/tohell/

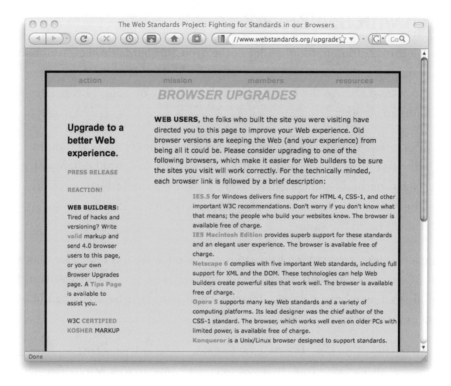

Figure 4.1. Redirection page for the Browser Upgrade Campaign

Like many other designers and developers at the time, I responded by publishing my own site with a CSS layout and valid markup in April 2001.

History Repeats

With the imminent release of Internet Explorer 8, we find ourselves in the very same position as we did back in 2001. The time for lobbying the browser makers to improve their support for web standards is over—for now, they have done their part. Now it's our turn.

As I write this, efforts such as Save the Developers[4] are already gearing up to encourage users of IE6 and IE7 to upgrade their browsers. Building that awareness is one part of the equation. The other is to give users a *reason* to upgrade, by using the features only available in up-to-date browsers in our designs—CSS tables, for instance.

---

[4] http://savethedevelopers.org/

As in 2001, we have several ways we can approach this process of gentle persuasion, and the most appropriate option will vary from project to project. Obviously, if we wanted to make the biggest impact possible, we could simply block old, out-of-date browsers from viewing our sites. That's a rather extreme approach, though, and not one you are likely to be able to justify, even on your own personal site—or not for another couple of years, at least.

No, most likely you'll want to let users of older browsers view some version of your site; the question is, *what* version should you allow them to see? What are your options?

Option 1: Ignore Older Browsers

The simplest option is to send older browsers—such as IE6 and IE7—the exact same site that up-to-date browsers are allowed to see, CSS tables and all. This is the approach we eventually hope to end up using in all our work, once the number of IE6 and IE7 users has dropped to a small enough fraction of our audience. Just as we now consider ourselves free to ignore obsolete browsers such as Netscape 4, we will one day be free to ignore IE7.

Chances are, however, that that day has not yet arrived.

The layout that we created in Chapter 2 looks like the screenshot in Figure 4.2 in all browsers that support CSS tables.

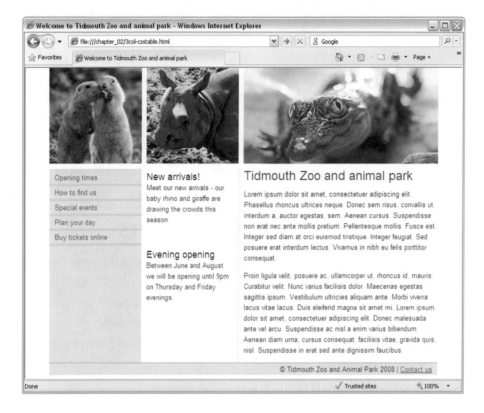

Figure 4.2. The layout in supported browsers

However, if we make no provisions for Internet Explorer 6 and 7, we'll see something like Figure 4.3 in those older browsers.

What we can see in IE6 and IE7 are the three columns stacked vertically, one on top of the other. As CSS tables aren't supported by the browser, these browsers ignore the instruction telling them to display the `div` elements as table cells. Therefore, they display them in the default style for `div` elements: as blocks displayed one after the other in source order.

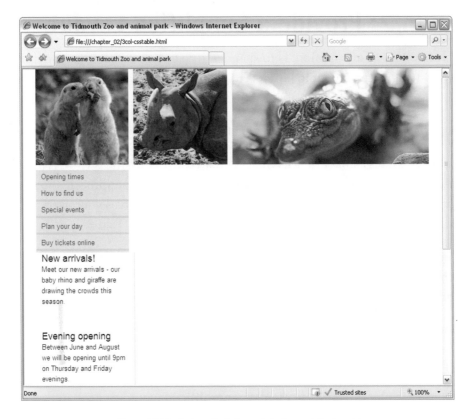

Figure 4.3. Vertical stack of elements in Internet Explorer 7

The page is usable enough, but it's obviously broken. With the number of people still using IE6 and IE7, this presentation is going to be a tough sell.

If you're designing for yourself and nobody else, this is an option you might want to consider—it'll certainly save you some time, and if you're looking to make a point, this is the most visible way to do it. Be sure to use a script like that on offer from the Save the Developers project,[5] to let users know why the page doesn't look right in their outdated browser, though.

For most projects, however, you'll probably need to consider making some provision for older browsers.

---

[5] http://savethedevelopers.org/

Option 2: Provide a Simplified Layout

The best option, in my opinion, is to spend a little extra time after you've finished your CSS-table-based layout to build a simplified layout using only the layout features supported by older browsers.

A simplified layout like this has two benefits:

■ It provides a lesser experience when compared with the site as viewed in an up-to-date browser, but it doesn't actually look broken. This approach allows the appearance of your site to remain professional, but still gives your users a gentle nudge to upgrade their browsers.

■ The simplified layout allows you to save yourself all that time it would take to achieve sophisticated designs using convoluted CSS layout techniques, such as absolute positioning, floated layout, and faux columns.

Let's see how this is done …

Adding a Style Sheet for IE6 and 7

For Internet Explorer 6 and 7 to display a simplified layout, we need to provide them with some different styling information. One option is to use conditional comments.

Conditional comments were introduced by Microsoft[6] in order to give web developers a way to target versions of Internet Explorer. While I have some misgivings about the insertion of code for the browser within comments—which are supposed to be ignored by the browser—they do provide a simple way to pass information that will be ignored by other browsers and non-targeted versions of Internet Explorer.

For example, if we want to include a style sheet for only Internet Explorer 6—a situation that is my most common use of conditional comments—we use the following markup:

---

[6] http://msdn.microsoft.com/en-us/library/ms537512(VS.85).aspx

```
<!--[if IE 6]>
<link rel="stylesheet" type="text/css" href="ie6.css" />
<![endif]-->
```

We'd typically put this style sheet after the main style sheet in the document, then overwrite any problematic CSS with rules for IE6 only in this special style sheet. The cascade approach dictates that if two style sheets in the document have the same selectors, the one that comes later in the document will be applied after the rules in the earlier style sheet, and will have the last word on how elements are displayed.

In this case, we want to add a style sheet for any version of Internet Explorer below IE8, so we use this conditional comment in which lt IE8 means *if less than IE8*:

3col-csstable-ie7simplified.html *(excerpt)*

```
<!--[if lt IE 8]>
<link rel="stylesheet" type="text/css"
    href="3col-csstable-ie7simplified.css" />
<![endif]-->
```

This condition is ideal, as when Internet Explorer 9 comes out we can safely assume it won't have dropped support for CSS tables. Therefore, this condition will still work—and it won't accidentally catch a newer browser than was available at the time of building the site. This block of code goes in the head of the document, after the original style sheet, as shown in Figure 4.4.

```
1  <!DOCTYPE html PUBLIC "-//W3C//DTD XHTML 1.0 Strict//EN"
2  "http://www.w3.org/TR/xhtml1/DTD/xhtml1-strict.dtd">
3  <html xmlns="http://www.w3.org/1999/xhtml" lang="en-US">
4    <head>
5      <title>Welcome to Tidmouth Zoo and animal park</title
6      ><meta http-equiv="content-type" content="text/html; charset=utf-8"/>
7      <link rel="stylesheet" type="text/css" href="3col-csstable.css"/>
8      <!--[if lt IE 8]>
9      <link rel="stylesheet" type="text/css" href="3col-csstable-ie7simplified.css"/>
10     <![endif]-->
11   </head>
12   <body>
13     <div id="wrapper">
14       <div id="header"></div>
15       <div id="main">
16         <div id="nav">
17           <ul>
18             <li><a href="#">Opening times</a></li>
19             <li><a href="#">How to find us</a></li>
20             <li><a href="#">Special events</a></li>
21             <li><a href="#">Plan your day</a></li>
22             <li><a href="#">Buy tickets online</a></li>
23           </ul>
24         </div>
```

Figure 4.4. The head of my document with the conditional comments in place

We create the new style sheet by saving the existing style sheet with a new name: **3col-csstable.oldbrowsers.css**. The selectors in the existing style sheet provide a useful starting point for our IE6 and 7 style sheet.

Now, we don't need to preserve *every* selector in this style sheet; many of the existing rules for styling text and simple aspects of the layout will work just fine in older browsers—we only need to override the rules for the elements that are set to display as tables, table rows, or table cells. So we can delete everything in the new style sheet other than those rules, which leaves the following CSS:

```css
#main {
  display: table;
  border-collapse: collapse;
}
#main .inner {
  display: table-row;
}
#nav {
  display: table-cell;
  width: 180px;
  background-color: #e7dbcd;
}
#extras {
  display: table-cell;
  padding-left: 10px;
  border-right: 1px dotted #d7ad7b;
  width: 180px;
}
#content {
  display: table-cell;
  width: 380px;
  padding-left: 10px;
}
```

Then, we merely edit these rules to make the changes needed for Internet Explorer versions less than version 8. The first step is to empty the `#main` and `#main .inner` rules:

```
                                    3col-csstable-ie7simplified.css (excerpt)

#main {
}
#main .inner {
}
```

We'll leave these selectors in place as a reminder, in case we need to come back and apply styles to the entire content area of the page. We don't need them to create our table and table row for now, though, so we can leave them as unstyled blocks (the default for divs).

Now, since we don't have a CSS table, we need to decide how we'll lay out the div elements nav, extras, and content. Each of these are CSS table cells in our table-based layout, but what do we do with them in our simplified layout?

Back in the section called "The Grid's the Thing" in Chapter 1, I explained that CSS was originally designed with the idea that every page would be a vertical stack of blocks. If we embrace this assumption in our simplified design, we should find the CSS code required to describe it very easy to write. Let's remove the display property values for each of these elements—they'll default to display: block—and set their width property back to auto so they span the full width of the page:

```
                                    3col-csstable-ie7simplified.css (excerpt)

#nav {
  width: auto;
}
#extras {
  width: auto;
  border-right: none;
  border-bottom: 1px dotted #d7ad7b;
}
#content {
  width: auto;
}
```

Since we're stacking the blocks vertically instead of horizontally, we've also moved the dotted border from the right side of the extras div to the bottom side. Figure 4.5 shows what the layout looks like in IE7 at this point.

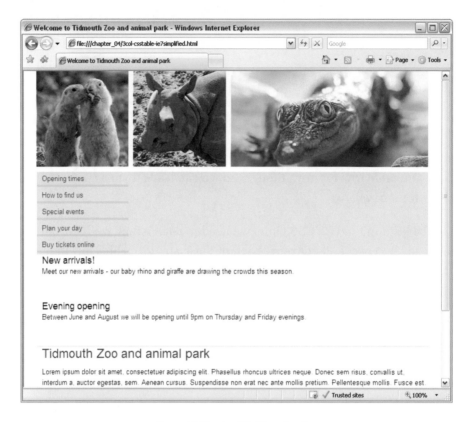

Figure 4.5. The simplified layout so far

The page is now a vertical stack of blocks, but the contents of those blocks still look as though they were designed to stack horizontally across the page. Let's add a few extra rules to our simplified layout style sheet to correct this issue.

It we look at the navigation menu, which in up-to-date browsers runs vertically down the left side, we can see that displaying it as a vertical list really doesn't work in this layout. It would be nice to stack those menu items horizontally across the page in our simplified layout, but again, we run into the problem that CSS wasn't designed to perform horizontal stacking of blocks.

We could fall back on our bag of tricks and use floats to perform the horizontal stacking, but remember that it's this kind of fragile hack we're trying to avoid with a simplified layout. Luckily, there is a much simpler option: display the list items as inline elements, so they flow across the page naturally—no stacking required!

3col-csstable-ie7simplified.css *(excerpt)*

```
#nav {
  width: auto;
  padding: 8px 0;
}
  ⋮
#nav li, #nav a:link, #nav a:visited {
  display: inline;
}
```

As the main style sheet has both the list items and the links within them displayed as blocks, we need to set `display: inline` on the list items, as well as both visited and unvisited links inside them. With a little extra padding on the `nav` div, we can even make the thick border below each of the links fit nicely inside our simplified layout.

The other aspect of the design that really isn't working in this simplified layout is the padding around the news items in `extras`. We can fix this easily with a final style rule:

3col-csstable-ie7simplified.css *(excerpt)*

```
#extras .box {
  padding: 0;
}
```

And we're done! Our completed, simplified layout is shown in Figure 4.6, as displayed by Internet Explorer 7.

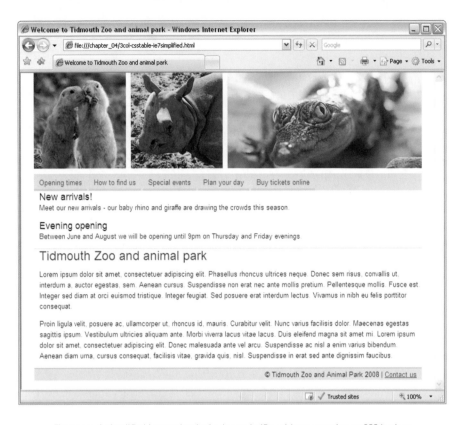

Figure 4.6. A simplified layout that looks decent in IE7, without resorting to CSS hackery

Option 3: Reproduce Your Layout with Older Techniques

Sometimes you'll have no choice but to support IE6 and 7 with the best design these browsers are able to display. Either you'll find yourself working for a client that insists the site must look exactly the same in every browser that you support, or you'll be building a site for an audience that, for whatever reason, contains a large segment of users with outdated browsers. Such situations should become less and less common over time, but for now at least you must be prepared for them.

What you need to do is reproduce your table-based layout as closely as possible using the features available in IE6 and 7. Again, we'll start by adding a conditional comment that adds an extra style sheet for versions of Internet Explorer older than IE8:

```
<!--[if lt IE 8]>
<link rel="stylesheet" type="text/css"
    href="3col-csstable-oldbrowsers.css" />
<![endif]-->
```

And again, we'll take as a starting point for **3col-csstable-oldbrowsers.css** the rules from **3col-csstable.css** that create CSS tables:

```
#main {
  display: table;
  border-collapse: collapse;
}
#main .inner {
  display: table-row;
}
#nav {
  display: table-cell;
  width: 180px;
  background-color: #e7dbcd;
}
#extras {
  display: table-cell;
  padding-left: 10px;
  border-right: 1px dotted #d7ad7b;
  width: 180px;
}
#content {
  display: table-cell;
  width: 380px;
  padding-left: 10px;
}
```

Now we can modify each of these rules to produce the layout we want in Internet Explorer 6 and 7:

3col-csstable-oldbrowsers.css *(excerpt)*

```
#main {
}
#main .inner {
}
```

Again, both the `#main` and `#main .inner` rules can be left empty, since the default unadorned blocks produced by these `div` elements will work just fine for our purposes.

`nav` is the very first column containing the navigation:

3col-csstable-oldbrowsers.css (excerpt)

```
#nav {
  float: left;
}
```

The `width` and `background-color` property values specified in the main style sheet can be left alone, but for IE6 and 7 we must add `float: left` to make this block into a column:

3col-csstable-oldbrowsers.css (excerpt)

```
#extras {
  float: left;
}
```

This will float the `div` to the left side of the page and allow the next column to come up alongside it. The same goes for the middle column, `extras`. Floating the box causes it to gain a layout—setting Internet Explorer 6 and 7's magical `hasLayout` property to `true`. We made mention of this concept back in the section called "Absolute Positioning" in Chapter 2.

Finally, we `float` the final column left as well. We'll also reduce the width of this column slightly to ensure there's room for it to float up against the other two columns, and not be forced to display underneath:

3col-csstable-oldbrowsers.css (excerpt)

```
#content {
  float: left;
  width: 370px;
}
```

The final step is to set the `footer div` to `clear: both` to make sure it stays below our floated columns:

```
                                          3col-csstable-oldbrowsers.css (excerpt)

#footer {
  clear: both;
}
```

The finished layout is shown in Figure 4.7.

Figure 4.7. The layout in Internet Explorer 7

The layout now looks reasonable in Internet Explorer 7; the columns are displaying alongside each other and it all holds together pretty well. The background doesn't extend down to the footer as it does in the tables version, but this doesn't prevent someone from using the site.

If you wanted to add the background in for IE6 and IE7 users, it actually isn't too difficult in this case. We can simply add a background image such as that shown in Figure 4.8 to one of the redundant wrapper `divs`, such as `main`.

Figure 4.8. The background image

3col-csstable-oldbrowsers.css *(excerpt)*

```css
#main {
  background-image: url(images/main-bg.gif);
  background-repeat: repeat-y;
}
```

This adds the background to the `main` `div` that contains all three columns and should create the faux columns effect described in Chapter 2.

At the same time, add `border-right: none` to the rule for the `extras` to remove the dotted right border, which is now replaced by the faux columns image:

3col-csstable-oldbrowsers.css *(excerpt)*

```css
#extras {
  float: left;
  border-right: none;
}
```

At this point, you won't see the faux columns effect when you view the layout in Internet Explorer 7. With all three columns floated, there's no non-floated content to hold open the `main` `div`, so it collapses down to nothing. Giving `main` a one-pixel red border, as shown in Figure 4.9, enables you to see what has happened.

Figure 4.9. The red line is the collapsed main div

Luckily, there's a fairly easy fix. Simply float main as well, which will force it to expand to contain the floated columns inside it:

3col-csstable-oldbrowsers.css *(excerpt)*

```
#main {
  float: left;
  width: 100%;
  background-image: url(main-bg.gif);
  background-repeat: repeat-y;
}
```

The finished layout should now be displayed correctly in IE7, as shown in Figure 4.10.

Figure 4.10. The layout in IE7 with the faux columns background in place

Here's the finished style sheet for IE6 and 7:

3col-csstable-oldbrowsers.css (excerpt)

```css
#main {
  float: left;
  width: 100%;
  background-image: url(images/main-bg.gif);
  background-repeat: repeat-y;
}
#main .inner {
}
#nav {
  float: left;
}
#extras {
  float: left;
  border-right: none;
```

```
}
#content {
  float: left;
  width: 370px;
}
#footer {
  clear: both;
}
```

But Why Not Stick with Floated Layouts?

If you're a professional web designer, perhaps you're reading this chapter with a certain degree of skepticism. Maybe most of your clients *do* insist on pixel-perfect rendering in IE6 and 7, and will continue to do so for some time.

Having read the third option above, you might wonder why anyone would bother using CSS tables, given they have to then create a fallback version using old-style floated layout techniques. Why not just use the float-based layout techniques you already know for *all* browsers?

This question really is the central issue of this book, so in this section we'll explore the reasons you should make the extra effort to adopt new layout techniques, rather than sticking with what you know.

Now It's Our Turn

For years, we've criticized Microsoft for holding back the Web by abandoning development of Internet Explorer while its competitors responded to our demands and added the new CSS features. With Internet Explorer 8, Microsoft has caught up. All the features we need to improve the Web with solid, reliable, and—most importantly—easy-to-learn page layout techniques are now available across all the major browsers.

If we don't start using those features now, *then* who's holding back the Web? The users who haven't upgraded their browsers? Until we build sites that take advantage of the new features added to the latest browsers, how can we expect those users to upgrade?

When we told Microsoft we needed it to improve Internet Explorer, we were making a bargain with the software giant: "You improve the browser to make our lives easier, and we'll build the sites that take full advantage of it, giving your users a reason to upgrade." Microsoft has done its part; now it's our turn.

Yes, embracing new CSS techniques while supporting older browsers involves some extra work, but this is something we've done before, and the Web benefited greatly. Back in 2001, web designers began to abandon HTML tables used for layout in favour of then-nascent CSS layout techniques, which were made possible by improvements in the newest browsers, including Internet Explorer 5.5. At the time, there were still plenty of Netscape 4 users around, and designers were forced to create separate versions of their sites for these users.

The designers of 2001 didn't have the benefit of conditional comments to ease this extra burden, but one by one they made the bold move to CSS layout. The result is that the vast majority of sites designed today use CSS layout, and benefit from the advantages it provides.

With the release of Internet Explorer 8, it's 2001 all over again.

Premium Design Elements

If we want to benefit from advances in browser support, at some point we have to decide that some browsers have limitations which mean they can't benefit from the full look and feel of the design we need to implement. That doesn't mean cutting those users off from being able to visit and use your site; it's just that the design isn't going to look the same for those users.

As an example, let's revisit the image gallery grid we developed in the section called "Making a Perfect Grid" in Chapter 2, shown here in Figure 4.11.

Figure 4.11. The grid using `display: table;`

Remember how well CSS tables work here, as we can make all the boxes in each row the same height, regardless of how much text is entered. To support Internet Explorer 7, we can add a couple of rules to float the boxes instead of using the table grid:

```
                                                csstable-grid-ie.css
.row {
  clear: both;
}
.image {
  float: left;
  margin: 2px;
}
```

The issue here will be that the backgrounds aren't as neat, but it degrades quite well, as you can see in Figure 4.12.

Figure 4.12. IE7 with the floated version of the grid

There really isn't a good way to emulate this type of layout without CSS tables. This grid effect is something that has been elusive until the advent of CSS tables, which is why you often see sites with captions spilling over the edges of boxes when the browser's text size is increased. The developer has assumed everyone has their text set to the same size, and fixed the height of the boxes to create this effect.

Greater Ease of Development

Floated and positioned CSS layout techniques have their problems, which can mean quite a bit of testing in different browsers—even in up-to-date browsers. The stability and reliability of table-based layouts was, for a long time, the main reason some designers chose to stick with HTML tables for layout, rather than embracing newer CSS techniques.

Using CSS tables for your layout will bring this stability to your CSS layout work. You'll waste a lot less time fixing mysterious bugs and inexplicable behavior in even the latest browsers.

If you're also able to use Option 1 (no fallback layout) or Option 2 (simplified fallback layout) described above, your testing burden will be reduced in browsers that don't support CSS tables as well. But even if you must resort to Option 3, fixing squirrelly layout bugs only in IE6 and 7 sure beats fixing bugs across the full range of browsers in use today!

I'm sure that I'm not the only designer working with CSS every day who experiences frustration over implementing my complex, grid-based layouts using current CSS that works across browsers.

As grid-based layout has made its transition from traditional media and onto the Web, often the only ways to implement these layouts using CSS are to add additional markup or to use a complicated mixture of CSS floats and positioning; neither of these were intended to create the kind of rich, visual interfaces that the modern Web demands.

While the (slow) work of the CSS working group includes new layout tools, these are some years away from becoming available. The table-related values for the CSS `display` property go some way to making my life happy, and as they're being implemented in the next version of Internet Explorer, they should make those other frustrated designers happier too.

—Andy Clarke[7]

---

[7] http://www.stuffandnonsense.co.uk/

Moving Forward

In this chapter, we discussed several approaches for supporting older browsers while embracing layout using CSS tables. Even though there are still a considerable number of users relying on browsers that don't support CSS tables, the time to begin using this technology in production is right now.

Still, even if you're excited about the new possibilities CSS tables bring to your layouts, you're bound to be amazed at what's around the corner. In the next and final chapter of this book, we'll take a look at what the future might hold for CSS. Specifically, we'll be concerning ourselves with some of the CSS3 properties that stand a good chance of eclipsing even CSS tables in adding creative freedom to the business of web design.

Chapter 5

The Road Ahead

Although it can seem as though browser development is moving at a glacial pace, a lot has happened in the past decade. In this chapter, we'll take a look at some of the concepts that are part of the CSS3 draft specification, and those that browsers have already implemented, giving us a chance to have a peek into the future of CSS.

The techniques described in this chapter are taken from working drafts of CSS3, and any of these aspects could change substantially before becoming a final recommendation. What is clear, however, is that the W3C is looking at new ways to solve the problems that exist in laying out our pages using CSS; some interesting proposals are being developed to help ease those difficulties.

By way of a quick clarification, CSS3 is the next version of CSS, currently being developed by the W3C. In any discussion surrounding CSS3, you'll likely come across references to the specification being "modularized." All this means is that the different parts of the specification have been split up into modules; for example, one module for selectors, another for positioning, and so on. Breaking the specification into modules allows different parts of the specification to progress and become an official recommendation at different times.

Therefore, browser vendors can begin implementing completed modules more quickly, without needing to wait for the entire specification to reach completion. As we'll see in this chapter, some modules are more advanced than others and even have working implementations in browsers that we can try out. Other modules are at a very early stage, so we can only describe what promises the current working draft is making for them. I hope that you will agree, after reading this chapter, that there are some very interesting innovations on the horizon for CSS!

CSS3 Multi-column Layout Module

First up, we'll look at the eagerly anticipated opportunity for developers to create newspaper-like columns in their layouts; I give you the CSS3 multi-column layout module.[1] In a multi-column layout, you have a single block of text that's formatted into multiple columns; the text flows down column one, then continues at the top of column two, and so on. Currently, if you have a block of content that you'd like to display in three even columns, you have to try to work out where to break the content and start the next column. The locations of column breaks are very difficult to predict when you're not formatting each page by hand; for example, this is the case with most database-driven web sites that generate pages dynamically.

With traditional layout techniques, we have to carefully tweak the column markup to achieve the effect we want. Here's some sample markup for a multi-column layout:

multi-column.html *(excerpt)*

```
<div class="wrapper">
  <div class="col1">
    <p>Lorem ipsum dolor sit amet, consectetuer adipiscing elit.
        Fusce porttitor porta magna. … Nullam
        pulvinar nisl viverra risus dapibus cursus.</p>
    <p>Aliquam tristique tristique massa. … Donec vestibulum
        elementum urna. Aenean convallis luctus lacus.</p>
  </div>
  <div class="col2">
    <p>Ut tincidunt turpis quis sem. … Sed pellentesque, neque
        ac iaculis congue, sapien est convallis nibh, eget
        posuere eros leo quis mauris.</p>
  </div>
```

---

[1] http://www.w3.org/TR/css3-multicol/

```
  <div class="col3">
    <p>Sed ullamcorper, elit eget dignissim blandit, … Donec
       eget massa. Nam eget est et nisl vestibulum iaculis.</p>
  </div>
</div>
```

In the above markup, we've had to manually place an even amount of text within each column. Here's the accompanying CSS:

multi-column.css *(excerpt)*

```
.wrapper {
  width: 80%;
}
.col1, .col2, .col3 {
  width: 30%;
  float: left;
  margin-right: 2%
}
```

We can achieve the effect shown in Figure 5.1 with careful tweaking of text in the three div elements and application of the above CSS. However, if any of the content changes we then have to reflow the whole thing; a less than satisfactory situation!

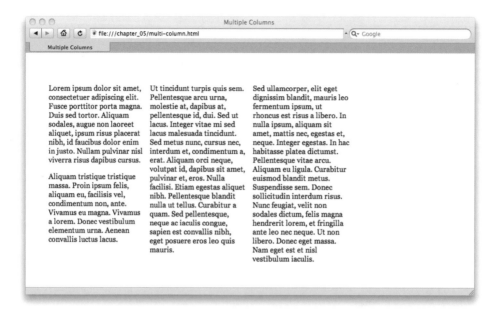

Figure 5.1. The effect after arranging the text by hand

The CSS3 multi-column module will allow you to divide a block of content into a specified number of equal-height columns. All we need to recreate our example above, as far as markup is concerned, is the following:

```
<div class="multi-wrapper">
  <p>Lorem ipsum dolor…</p>
  <p>Aliquam tristique…</p>
  <p>Ut tincidunt turpis…</p>
  <p>Sed ullamcorper…</p>
</div>
```

In the above markup all we need is a parent block element, into which we then place all the content paragraphs. The following CSS will create our columns:

```
.multi-wrapper {
  width: 80%;
  column-count: 3;
  column-gap: 1em;
}
```

Specifying a `column-count` value for the containing `div` will automatically turn the block of content into three equal-height columns. The `column-gap` property is used to set the width of the gutter between columns. In the case of a fluid layout, resizing the browser window will cause the columns to reflow; the browser works out the size of the columns and where to break the content. If your page content is dynamic, as long as the content is placed within the correct container, the browser will do all the work for you.

Happily, we can put this module through its paces—it's been implemented in Mozilla Firefox since version 1.5 and Safari since version 3. In order to see it in action, you'll need to prefix the properties with a vendor extension identifier: `-moz-` for Mozilla Firefox, and `-webkit-` for Safari:

css3-multi-column.css (excerpt)

```
.multi-wrapper {
  width: 80%;
  -moz-column-count: 3;
  -moz-column-gap: 1em;
  -webkit-column-count: 3;
  -webkit-column-gap: 1em;
  column-count: 3;
  column-gap: 1em;
}
```

If you open the example in Safari, you'll see the contents formatted evenly into three columns, as shown in Figure 5.2.

Figure 5.2. The columns as displayed in Safari 3.1

If you add more content or perhaps an image, the text will reflow to remain evenly distributed across the columns, as you can see in Figure 5.3.

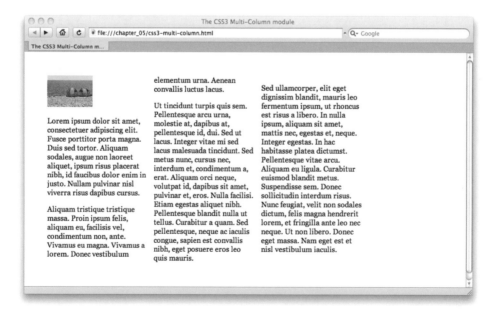

Figure 5.3. The content reflows automatically

Multiple Equal-width Columns

Another way to break your text into columns is to specify the width that you'd like your columns to be; the browser will create more or fewer columns depending on the amount of available space. All we need to do is a quick CSS modification:

```
                                        css3-multi-column-width.css (excerpt)

.multi-wrapper {
  width: 80%;
  -moz-column-width: 10em;
  -moz-column-gap: 1em;
  -webkit-column-width: 10em;
  -webkit-column-gap: 1em;
  column-width: 10em;
  column-gap: 1em;
}
```

The `column-width` property allows us to specify our desired column width—10em in the above CSS excerpt. Figure 5.4 shows the result in Firefox: a four-column layout. However, if we reduce the window size, the content is reformatted. Figure 5.5 demonstrates Firefox's reduction of the content to two columns when we reduce the width of the browser window.

Figure 5.4. This screen width fits four columns in Firefox 3

Figure 5.5. As we drag in the browser window, the content displays as two columns

Other Multi–column Layout Properties

The following list details the other properties defined in the CSS3 multi-column layout module, along with their equivalent vendor specific extensions where appropriate:

columns

This shortcut property allows the specification of the `column-count` and `column-width` properties in one declaration.

column-rule-color

This property works like `border-color` and allows the color of the rule between columns to be specified. You can also use `-moz-column-rule-color` in Firefox 3.1 and up, and `-webkit-column-rule-color` in Safari 3 and up.

column-rule-style

Like `border-style`, this property allows the style of the column rule to be specified. You can also use `-moz-column-rule-style` in Firefox 3.1 and up, and `-webkit-column-rule-style` in Safari 3 and up.

column-rule-width

Just like `border-width`, this property allows the specification of the column rule width. `-moz-column-rule-width` is available in Firefox 3.1 and up, and `-webkit-column-rule-color` in Safari 3 and up.

column-rule

This shorthand property acts in the same way as the `border` property, specifying all the column rule properties in one declaration; for example, `column-rule: 1px solid #000;`. You can also use `-moz-column-rule` in Firefox 3.1 and up, and `-webkit-column-rule` in Safari from version 3.

column-span

You can use this property to specify that an element should span two or more columns.

column-balance

This property takes a value of `balance` or `auto`, and is used to specify that the browser should try to balance the columns or fill them sequentially.

column-break-before and column-break-after

For paged media, these properties are used to specify where columns should break when running onto another page. They take the values `always`, `avoid`, and `auto`.

 Using Vendor-specific Extensions

Many browser vendors have implemented extensions to the CSS Specification. Vendor-specific extensions allow browser vendors to experiment with implementations of parts of the specification that aren't yet at Recommendation level, and so are subject to change. The use of the dash (`-moz-` for the Mozilla Foundation, `-ms-` for Microsoft, `-o-` for Opera, and `-webkit-` for the Webkit Open Source Project used by Safari) is the W3C-recognized way for extensions to be implemented. By using this method, a browser vendor can be sure that the CSS Specification will never include a property with this name.

An excellent introduction to browser-specific extensions can be found in the SitePoint CSS Reference.[2]

---

[2] http://reference.sitepoint.com/css/vendorspecific/

CSS3 Grid Positioning Module

CSS properties that deal with the layout of items on a grid are encapsulated in the CSS3 Grid Positioning Module.[3] As grid-based layouts become ever more popular, designers struggle to make CSS layouts behave within the constraints of a grid. As we've seen in this book, having CSS tables in our toolkit will help us create grid-based layouts right now; the Grid Positioning module, as well as the Template Layout module we'll look at next, really push layout control to the next level. Imagine being able to define a grid for your page, then snap elements to that grid! This is what the CSS3 Grid Positioning module is trying to make possible.

At the time of writing there are no current browser implementations of the CSS3 grid positioning module, so we have to take a look at the working draft to see what's being proposed.

The `grid-columns` and `grid-rows` Properties

The new properties introduced in this module are `grid-columns` and `grid-rows`. These allow the designer to create an explicit grid within a containing element—which could be the `body`, or a `div`, or other element as required. So, if you wanted a seven-column grid where each column is `10em` wide, with a `1em` gap between the columns, you'd specify this using the following CSS rule:

```
body {
   grid-columns(10em,1em,10em,1em,10em,1em,10em,1em,10em,1em,10em,
      1em,10em;
}
```

The grid layout that would be created by the above CSS is depicted in Figure 5.6.

---

[3] http://www.w3.org/TR/css3-grid/

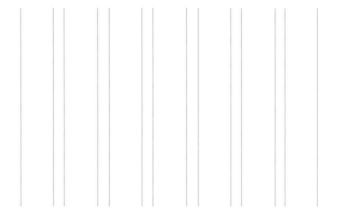

Figure 5.6. Seven columns with gaps between them

Since this is a repeating pattern, we can also use the following notation instead of specifying all of the columns individually:

```
body {
  grid-columns(10em,1em)[7];
}
```

The [7] in square brackets after the column values means "repeat this pattern seven times."

Likewise, `grid-rows` gives you the ability to specify the number of rows and their heights in your grid.

Creating a Grid with Columns and Column-gap Properties

According to the working draft, we could also create our grid using the columns and column-gap properties, like so:

```
body  {
  columns: 7;
  column-gap: 10px;
}
```

This CSS would give us a grid of seven columns with a ten-pixel gap between them, and the columns would evenly stretch to the width of the container. In the case of a body with no width applied, they'd evenly stretch if the window was resized.

Positioning Elements on the Grid: the gr Value

Of course, once you've created a grid, you'll want to be able to position items along the grid lines. This is where grid positioning really comes into its own.

The Grid Positioning Module introduces a new length value: gr. This unit of length is to be used to specify how many grid units an element occupies. So the following CSS would cause the element with an id of promo to span four grid units, and be positioned one grid unit from the left:

```
#promo {
  position: absolute;
  left: 1gr;
  width: 4gr;
}
```

The result of this rule is shown in Figure 5.7. You'll notice that the 4gr value for the width of the element includes the columns we specified as gaps.

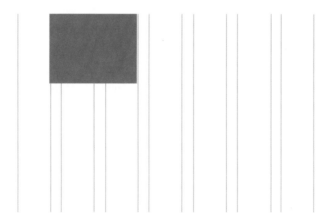

Figure 5.7. The diagram showing the position of the element

There are several illustrated examples in the current working draft for this module, as well as further information about how it might be used. The working draft is worth a read, if you're interested in where CSS might be taking us in the future—and it's one of the more readable CSS3 documents.

CSS3 Template Layout Module

The CSS3 Template Module,[4] previously referred to as the *Advanced Layout Module*, introduces the concept of templates within CSS. It's also an alternative layout method to the Grid Positioning Module for positioning elements to a grid or other layout. As with grid positioning, this module is still in an early stage of development, and as such there are no current browser implementations. The specification is likely to change prior to becoming a full W3C Recommendation.

The latest working draft of this module introduces the concept:

> This specification is part of level 3 of CSS ("CSS3") and contains features to describe layouts at a high level, meant for tasks such as the positioning and alignment of "widgets" in a graphical user interface or the layout grid for a page or a window, in particular when the desired visual order is different from the order of the elements in the source document.

The Template Layout Module aims to enable developers to create a template with slots in which to place the different elements. So rather than absolute positioning, which requires you to position elements using coordinates, you'd be able to command "place the navigation into slot A, and the main content into slot B"—very nice indeed, no?

Setting up the Template

Templates are created using the `display` property. Just as we saw with CSS tables, layout templates can be used for the whole layout or just a smaller element within a layout. For example, the following markup defines an unordered list with a `class` of `box`:

---

[4] http://www.w3.org/TR/css3-layout/

```
<ul class="box">
  <li>List item One</li>
  <li>List item Two</li>
  <li>List item Three</li>
</ul>
```

We'd like to display the list as three columns, and we'll use the template layout properties to achieve this end. To set up the three-column template, we use the `display` property with a value of `"abc"`, a letter for each template slot. This is, I'm sure you'll agree, a bit of an odd departure from the usual use of the `display` property; however, each letter simply represents one slot in the template:

```
.box {
  display: "abc";
}
```

Positioning Elements into the Slots

This module uses the `position` property to place elements into the slots. A letter that corresponds to the slot into which the element goes is used as the value for the `position` property, instead of the current keyword values, such as `absolute` and `relative`, that we're used to. We'll place our list items into their slots like so:

```
.box li {
  position: a;
}
.box li + li {
  position: b;
}
.box li + li + li{
  position: c;
}
```

The above CSS puts the first list item into slot a, the second into slot b, and the third into slot c. The result is shown in Figure 5.8.

List item One	List item Two	List item Three

Figure 5.8. Positioning into slots

One important point to note about this module is that, unlike CSS tables, you'll have complete control over the source order of your markup. You could display these list items in any order you like; the first item can go into slot b and the second into slot c, for example.

CSS3 templates also allow far more complex grids to be defined. While each letter specified in the string value for the display property represents a slot, you can specify multiple strings to represent rows. Here's a rule that specifies a grid of two rows with three columns:

```
body {
  display: "abc"
           "def";
}
```

You can also specify slots that span columns or rows using repetition; here, we specify that slot a should span three columns:

```
body {
  display: "aaa"
           "bcd";
}
```

CSS3 templates can be even more complex than that. We don't have enough room in this book to speculate on all the possibilities, but we'll conclude this section with an exciting example that demonstrates the real power of templates:

```
body {
  display: "a.b.c" /2em
           "a.d.e"
           5em 1em * 1em 10em;
}
```

Along with the letters, you can also include one or more dots (.) to indicate whitespace—that no elements can be displayed, as we've done above. We've also specified the height of the first row and the column widths. What the above rule creates is a two-row, five-column grid. The first row has a height of 2em. The first column is 5em wide and spans both rows; the second column is a 1em wide whitespace column, as is the fourth column. The last column is 10em wide. The central column has a flexible width, which is specified by an asterisk (*). This way, we achieve a level of layout control previously unheard of with CSS.

 Having a Virtual Go with JavaScript

As people start to get more interested in these modules, it's likely that we'll see more attempts to emulate them using JavaScript, such as the ALMcss plugin available from http://www.cesaracebal.com/research/thesis/almcss/.

If you like playing with these concepts, such emulators can certainly be a great way to bring them to life—although I wouldn't advise using them for production work!

As with the grid positioning module, the template layout module is in an early stage of development. The working draft contains more examples and up-to-date information as to how this module might eventually take shape. If you're interested in CSS3, do go and look at the examples in the working drafts; they are often far easier to understand than you might expect, as they aim to describe how something would work in practice. It may seem a bit complicated at first read, but a lot of that is because working in this way is quite a mental shift after being used to pushing things around using positioning and floating as we do currently.

If these examples have piqued your interest in the development of CSS3, a great site to visit and add to your RSS reader is css3.info.[5] This site contains up-to-the-

---

[5] http://www.css3.info/

minute information about the status of different modules, and the state of browser support.

Everything You Know about CSS Is Wrong

So we come to the end of our look at how, in a sense, everything you know about CSS is wrong. The support that Internet Explorer 8 will bring for CSS tables is just the beginning. It's an ironclad certainty that the way we lay out sites will change—how fast that change happens remains to be seen. However, by keeping your techniques up to date and not expecting life to remain the same, you can ensure that you're not left behind as techniques and support move on.

Recalling the history of CSS earlier in this book reminds me of just how brief is our history. While we might feel that certain buggy browsers have been around and will be around forever and ever, the reality is that "forever" is only a year or two away. To be a web designer or developer, and to be good at what you do, means accepting that change is rapid and constant. We all have to keep reading, keep trying out new techniques, and be ready to start using them as soon as browser technology catches up with us.

We all know how frustrating it can be when you have a project that really could do with multi-column layout right now, or when you're champing at the bit to be able to lay page elements out to a grid! However, playing around with browser-specific implementations can be fun, and keeps you right up to date with the new specifications. Reading working drafts and trying to figure out how implementations will work might not be everyone's idea of bedtime reading, but it brings you closer to the work that's being done to design the CSS of the future. Once we do start to see browser implementations, rather than complaining about having to learn something new, you'll be among those crowing, "At last we can do this!"

Index

THE CSS ANTHOLOGY

101 ESSENTIAL TIPS, TRICKS & HACKS

BY **RACHEL ANDREW**
2ND EDITION

THE ART & SCIENCE OF CSS

BY **CAMERON ADAMS**
JINA BOLTON
DAVID JOHNSON
STEVE SMITH
JONATHAN SNOOK

CREATE INSPIRATIONAL STANDARDS-BASED WEB DESIGN

THE PRINCIPLES OF
BEAUTIFUL
WEB DESIGN

BY JASON BEAIRD

DESIGN BEAUTIFUL WEB SITES USING THIS SIMPLE STEP-BY-STEP GUIDE

SIMPLY
JAVASCRIPT

BY **KEVIN YANK**
& CAMERON ADAMS

EVERYTHING YOU NEED TO LEARN JAVASCRIPT FROM SCRATCH